ALL THE LITTLE CHILDREN
NEED TO COME HOME

CA Coder

DEDICATION

This book is lovingly dedicated to my son
Todd Clifford Coder
1984-2010

PROLOGUE

*W*hisperings among the wind signaled the coming changes. Tiny footsteps clamored daintily above the clouds in the evening sky. Nervous giggles and the flapping of excited wings alerted the Elders, the older angels who had completed their journey on earth well into "old age," that the little ones were rushing towards the edge of the darkened clouds to peek at the earth below. They jostled among themselves to find a place along the puffy borders to peek for the coming New One, delighted in seeing fireflies dancing in the mist below.

The angels' joy to welcome the One was innocent and genuine. Their own time on earth had been brief. Someone was going to join them, that's all they knew. For these precious ones, this was a Heavenly place where everyone laughed and played, and love was the only word whispered in their ears.

The New One would be greeted by a cacophony of excited wings; he would be baffled and disoriented as he realized where he was. The Elders smiled sadly as they watched the little angels welcome him, knowing there would be shock and anger, denial and questioning of faith from those he left behind on Earth. Before acceptance, those below would go to the abyss of the heart, prepared to jump into the absolute comfort of oblivion. The Elders were prepared. They would provide silent words of comfort to those eft behind to find the will to step into a new future, without their beloved by their side. They would listen and answer their prayers. They would guide into Heaven those who could not live without to join their loved one as well.

CHAPTER 1

THE FIRST DAY

The morning sun peeked through the trees as another beautiful Friday began. Alice returned from taking her neighbor to work, and before she went to wake her youngest son, she put on a pot of coffee. She leaned over the sink and cranked open the kitchen window. The easy breeze of autumn brushed her face as she gazed out at the myriad of colors dabbing throughout her back yard. Smiling, she closed her eyes and enjoyed the moment.

This was going to be a *perfect* day.

Alice was looking forward to going to a matinee with her youngest son, Todd, to celebrate his twenty-sixth birthday this past August. It had been so long since they had gone anywhere together as a family, which was always a time precious to her. He found out just last night that there was an emergency in the family-owned business where he worked his full-time job, and they were closed until Monday. He had almost two full days before going to his part-time job early Saturday morning. In the past, knowing he didn't have to work in the morning, Todd would have gone out to a local sports bar. Instead, he chose to stay in and planned to take full advantage of the welcomed break. He had asked Alice if she would join him tomorrow for an early matinee, and she immediately said yes.

Alice crinkled her brow and her eyes teared as she remembered that day, over three years ago, when she woke up at 3AM, peeked out the window, and saw that Todd's car was not in the driveway. She had spoken to him just before midnight and he had been on his way home; that had been hours ago.

When his cellphone went directly to voicemail both times she tried, her heart began to pound and she tried to calm the desperate thoughts racing through her mind. She noticed the flashing blue and red lights bouncing around the walls of her bedroom as the patrol car creeped down the driveway, and her heart began to pound with her racing fears. Her husband was sleeping soundly under the bedcovers, and she decided not to wake him. She took a breath and went downstairs.

The coffee maker beeped into her musings. Glancing at the kitchen clock, she had a few more minutes before she would wake her son, and they'd get ready for the movie. She poured a mug of steaming coffee and turned to rest her back against the sink. She blinked back tears, remembering that other early morning that seemed so long ago.

The moon peeked brightly through the side windows of her front door. Before she opened the door, she instinctively dropped to her knees and bowed her head in prayer. From being just a year into a program of recovery from an alcohol problem, she had learned two things. First, she prayed that Todd, or whoever they were here for, would be all right. Then she did something she had never done before. She prayed that whatever had happened, what-ever they told her, God would give her the strength to help her through. Two officers were standing there, awkwardly silent. She spoke first.

"Is it Todd?"

An incredible calm crept over her as she listened to them explain. Todd's car had gone airborne across the median on Old Bridge Road and knocked out a metal light pole, dragging it over

500 feet and almost into the oncoming traffic. He was flown to Inova Fairfax hospital in critical condition. They asked if she needed a ride, if she needed to call anyone. She replied that her husband was home and they would leave immediately.

"Is he all right? Will he be all right?" She noticed the glances between the two officers, and one said gently," He was awake and he was talking."

Alice closed the door and went upstairs to wake her husband, Ben. She quietly explained that Todd had been in an accident and they needed to go to the hospital. She splashed cool water on her face and neck, under her arms, before jumping into the clothes she had worn yesterday. Ben was already at the door. She grabbed her keys, but Ben took them from her, saying he would drive.

They drove North on I-95 through the quiet morning, passing little traffic. Alice sat leaning forward, hands folded, rocking back and forth. Neither spoke as they made the twenty-minute trip that seemed to last a thousand miles. Soon, they were walking into the emergency room at Fairfax Hospital, where her son lay on a gurney, neck in a brace, a bloody gash along his forehead.

Ben went to speak with doctors and Alice went to her son. She picked back strands of hair that stuck in the gash on his forehead, and took his hand. She showed no fear as she smiled down at him and whispered, "Hey, Todd."

"I'm sorry, Mom," he said, and she said to him the words that she would believe throughout his recovery.

"You're going to be fine."

"Hey!" Todd suddenly yelled, trying to look over his shoulder at the group of people standing nearby.

"Hey, quit talking about me as if I'm not here!"

Alice leaned towards him, brushing back his hair.

"Todd," she whispered. "They aren't talking about you." He focused on her again, and said quietly," I'm sorry, Mom. I just didn't want to get a third ticket." His eyes softened as he said the words.

Alice swallowed the empathy she immediately felt for him. She knew her son. He was a kind and thoughtful young man who was trying to get help for his drinking problem. Twenty-three years old, he thought, was too young to have a problem-until the second DUI. He decided he should get help and just this past Wednesday they had gone to a therapist schooled in "alcohol problems."

Each day they went back, the doctor prescribed more medications, and diagnosed him as Bi-Polar. The doctor had asked Todd if he always felt depressed and then agitated, with mood swings. Todd looked at Alice and said yes. Then the therapist asked Alice about the mood swings. Being in early recovery herself, she responded that just since he started drinking.

As Alice remembered that meeting, she leaned against the sink, glancing at the clock. She had a few more minutes before waking Todd up for the day. She felt grateful they stopped seeing that professional after the accident. She knew nothing about true alcoholism and the conflicting affects it had on one's psyche and personality.

When the psychiatrist who had evaluated Todd in the hospital after the accident called her, he asked her about the diagnosis of Bi-Polar and depression. Alice told him it was only the past two years, since leaving college. He agreed.

"I think he's an alcoholic," he had suggested. "Probably depressed, but not Bi-Polar. He should be in a program for alcoholics."

Alice agreed and it was after his third hospitalization that both she and Todd felt the first doctor had over medicated him from the start. As far as Alice was concerned, the increased medications led to a feeling of euphoria and Todd naturally felt it would be all right to have just one drink. A big mistake made by both the doctor, her son, and herself as well. She promised herself that she would research more about alcoholism; barely sober over a year herself, she was still learning about this disease and other addictions as well.

Within that next year, she would become almost an "expert" at addictions and alcoholism. Both changed normal human beings into Jekyll and Hyde; all the behaviors of an alcoholic in early recovery could be curious examples of all sorts of psychological behaviors. She had bought "The Pill Book" so she would understand all the medications he had been given by the 'specialist'. He left the hospital minus a few.

Alice had asked the attending physician that night if he believed in God. She said she did and that this was a miracle. He had nodded, taking her hands.

"I do believe in God, and yes this is a miracle. He survived."

Todd came home after four days, but within the next four weeks he would endure two emergency surgeries. He had developed a hematoma on the brain and the cervical vertebrae were collapsing. After ten days back home, he again underwent surgery to clear a staph infection that developed along the scar from where they had opened his skull and they had to operate again, making certain the infection was not inside the skull. Within another few days, he was stabilized enough to go home.

Todd's recovery was slow, but over the next three years, he doggedly pursued getting better. When he felt well enough, he had applied for part time jobs. Because of the effects of the brain injury and having his neck in a brace, he would be let go from each one, but he never gave up. Some people had suggested that he might qualify for disability, but he was determined to see if he could get better on his own. Through time and dedication, his thoughts became clearer, and the tremors eventually went away. Alice began to study the brain after injuries and encouraged him along the way. She felt the one saving grace was that Todd had never lost consciousness. His mind had stayed alert throughout the accident.

Alice exhaled quietly, as she thought about those years of recovery and how he never gave up. He not only had two jobs now, but he was smiling and happy and hanging out with his brother, Adam and friends again. She could tell that his body, mind, and spirit we re beginning to heal. She blinked back tears as her heart filled with pride for her son's fortitude to get better. He wouldn't give up. Once, months after his accident, he had asked her if he would ever recover completely. Alice smiled now, as she did then, when she gave him her usual response.

"Of course, you will. God's got this. He told me so." With a wink and a smile, she realized those simple words had great power. He believed her. Todd was determined to finish his last year of college, play baseball, and find his future. He was the happiest she had seen him in a while, completely at ease with his past; confident in his future. Everything was perfect.

Alice refilled her mug with coffee and poured a cup for him.

The last thing he said to her before he went to bed last night was, "You don't mind getting me up?"

"Nope. Not at all," she had replied, and she gave a 'thumbs up' signal. He smiled as he left the room. It was that wonderful 'Todd' smile, that told her he was at peace with the world. She knew she would never forget that smile.

Upstairs, Alice elbowed Todd's door open, turning first to the TV, which was on rather loud. That's strange, she thought. He never sleeps with the TV on. Setting the mugs on the TV stand, she reached for the remote and turned it off.

"Todd, your TV is kind of loud. Did you sleep with it that loud?"

She turned to her son, with a happiness of the day swelling in her heart, ready to see him snuggled on his stomach, leg hanging, jiggling his foot, beginning to wake up.

Instead, she saw her son laying in bed, facing the ceiling, as if he had just sat down and fallen asleep.

Her heart stopped.

Todd was flat on his back, arms to his side, eyes wide open. Her words froze in midair as she struggled to comprehend what was happening.

In that instant, she felt the air sucked out of the room. Struggling to breathe, she climbed onto the bed and wrapped her arms around him. Her mournful wail filled that quiet, carefree morning as her tears spilled on his hair, trying to force life back into him. She cried out, "God, what did I do?" Shock and confusion clouded her mind. She had always tried to be a good person, she had bargained with God, so she would never have to bury her child. In this moment, she thought somehow, she failed.

Holding her son's lifeless body tightly to her chest, her sobs filled the room. As she touched him, she startled at his warm back and heard a gurgle come from his throat.

Desperate hope rushed her mind against everything she saw to be true. She told her husband to call 911 as they gently moved him to the floor.

He's still alive, she thought against everything she saw to the contrary. God worked a miracle years ago. She believed he could work one now.

CHAPTER 2
ABOVE THE ROOM

It was the strangest feeling Todd ever had. He was being pulled into a small ocean current, the ripple of each wave carrying him slowly above his room. He smiled as he looked around below, thinking this was just some weird dream. He ducked his head as he neared the ceiling fan, but didn't feel the bump of the blade at all. He chuckled as he noticed how his room looked from up here. It was pretty messy, with clothes thrown casually over everything. He heard soft whisperings around him, yet he was more intrigued by what was happening in his bedroom below.

He saw his mother come into the room and turn towards his TV, saying something about why it was so loud. Todd didn't think it was too loud. From where he was in this dream, he could hardly hear anything at all. An intense wave of sadness filled the room as he watched his mother turn to his bed, saying his name.

"Todd...."

A shiver went through his body when he heard how she said his name. A curious tingle spread throughout him as his mom climbed onto his bed below, reaching to hold someone who was lying there, very still. Todd recognized the red silk shorts and white National's top the person was wearing. His heart beat faster as he realized the person cradled in his mother's arms was himself. He looked as if he was simply asleep.

But he wasn't. He was here, above the room, and he was dreaming. He had to be. He felt his mother's touch, ever so slightly, on his cheek. He watched her wrap her arms around his body, and he *felt* her holding him tightly, even as he looked down at her.

Wake up, he told himself. *Wake up!*

When she looked up at the ceiling, he thought she could see him. He smiled at her, but she looked right through him as her tears spilled onto his face below. He touched his cheek. He could *feel* her tears.

What was he doing down there on the bed, when he was up here? And why was he up here, when he should be down there?

He struggled to understand, wiggled to move.

Why won't he wake up?

Silence thundered through the room and into the morning air as he watched his mother, her mouth wide open, as she struggled to take a breath that would not come and he swallowed against the panic that raced in his thoughts.

The air around him felt cold. He shut his eyes against the fear that was pulsing through his body, shutting out the voices whispering all around.

He reached towards his mother, trying to tell her he was right here, that everything was going to work out. He experienced the peculiar sensation of floating down to touch her shoulder.

The silence shattered as he heard his mother cry, "Oh, God, no! No! What did I do?"

"What *did* you do?"

His father was standing in the doorway, hands braced against the sides. His eyes were bleary and his face was scrunched in disbelief.

Why is his dad yelling at his mom?

Sadness welled up inside him, and his heart settled into a soft imperceptible rhythm as he tried to listen to the whispers around

him. It seemed important to understand what the voices were trying to say, but he was entranced by what he saw happening below.

His father was dialing 911, and for an instant, he *knew* he felt
his mother's arms as they both lowered him down to the floor.
Nothing was making any sense. He fought back the troubling
panic that was beginning to engulf his body. Still, the whispers
surrounded him, soothing, telling him things would be all right.
Come here. It's okay. There's nothing you can do. It will be all right.

It's time.

Todd watched his mom put her head against his chest and
begin pumping. He could barely hear his father speaking into
the phone, and then saying, "The lady wants to hear you
counting."

Todd smiled when he heard his mom call back, "I *am* counting.
Tell her I know CPR!" When she began counting louder so the lady
on the phone could hear, Todd chuckled, remembering.

She had just completed a Red Cross course a few days ago and
she had pretended to practice on him. Todd smiled again as he
watched her continue to count, not giving up until the paramedics
came into the room.

It was only then, that Todd realized he was the only one
smiling.

The actions below him moved forward quickly and he blinked
tears that were not there as reality began to creep over him. With
one last prayer, he squeezed his eyes tight as he begged himself to
wake up.

"I don't like this movie..." He remembered saying those words
when he was a little boy, whenever a scary part would come on. "I
just don't like this movie!" His mother would quickly change the
channel or take him out of the room to distract him.

He repeated that same phrase now, and a lump formed in his
throat when he realized he was continuing to remember things
that had happened long ago.

He felt a heaviness fill the room as he began to understand the tone of the voices whispering all around. He had heard those whispers three years ago as he was airlifted after his accident. At the time, he thought it was the emergency crew trying to keep him from shutting his eyes. He had been awake the whole time. But the words were different that time. They were whispering it was *not* his time. He would survive.

Now, they were whispering ever so softly that it *was* time.

His time. Now.

Panic set in and a deep sorrow filled his heart as he realized this was the greatest of nightmares.

He was dying.

In a few moments, even as his mother tried to breathe life into him, he began to feel weak.

He made one last effort to go back into his body.

Immediately, he was lying flat on the floor as the paramedics asked his mom to step away. She leaned over him and kissed his forehead, and with that touch, he felt the embrace of a hundred unseen arms gently pulling him up to where he now belonged. With all his effort and all his love, he looked up into the face of his mother, haloed in light.

Mom, mommy, Mama Dukes.

That horrible feeling of loss engulfed him. He ached inside knowing now how much he would miss his mom, his dad, his brother, and all of his family and friends. With a deep awareness of what had just happened, he knew that he would miss life itself.

As he began to drift above, he saw one of the medics look at his watch and call the time of death. He heard his father, who had been standing at the door, yell out, "Oh, no, no, no! My God no!"

Todd watched his mother lift her head towards where he lay on the ground and as he tried to sit up, he looked at her and smiled.

He thought he saw her smile back. As Todd began to drift above his body, into the light of the morning sun, he heard an unfamiliar sound coming from his father as he stumbled down the hall, bracing himself against the walls.

Todd had never before heard or seen his father cry.

CHAPTER 3

ALICE

Alice was on her knees in the doorway, head lowered, praying so intensely that her mind went numb. She heard Ben cry out and looked up at the medic, who was checking his watch. She felt a lump in her throat when she looked at her son, lying so still beneath the window. His face seemed to shine as the morning light streamed in through the glass.

"He looks so peaceful," Alice whispered.

"Yes, ma'am, he does," one of the medics replied, nodding.

Alice stood up and walked down the hall. At the top of the stairs, she leaned against the wall and then slowly slid down to the floor. She began to shiver as she heard Ben moving around downstairs in the family room. She tucked her knees to her chest and wrapped her arms around them, holding herself tightly. The medic who had spoken to her earlier sat down beside her. He talked quietly, asking her questions about her son.

She answered in whispers. "No, he was happy. He had just gone to the doctor yesterday because he was having a hard time sleeping. Jittery. No, he had been sober for several weeks." She felt goosebumps travel down her arms and legs.

"I feel him," she whispered.

"I hear that happens sometimes," he replied, calmly.

She sighed deeply and looked at the young medic sitting beside her. He looked as young as Todd.

"I'm okay," she said to him. She realized he had been keeping her from going into shock, and she appreciated that. For a moment, her mind went blank, and her heart beat so quickly she felt like it would burst through her chest. Blinking to stop the tears, she realized she was still breathing.

"I have to call his brother," she said, quietly. The medic helped her up, and she went downstairs to her husband, who was standing at the bottom of the stairs, looking up at her with tear worn eyes.

"We have to tell Adam."

They stood there together, but each were alone in their thoughts.

"I'll call him," Ben said, and turned away.

Ben's eyes were blurry and his body reeked of alcohol. After another few months of sobriety, he had started drinking again last night. He was sitting to do taxes for the past year, and for an alcoholic, that was easily a reason to drink. She knew. As a recovering alcoholic herself, there is always a 'reason to drink.'

Alice watched as he called their oldest son. Ben seemed alert and resolute. They say that shock can make you instantly sober. At least for the moment.

"Are you at home?" and then "Where is Lindsay? You need to come home."

He listened for a second and then replied," Todd."

Alice heard his voice crack as he said Todd's name. She moved behind him and laid her head against his back. She did not feel judgment. It did not matter. She knew in her heart that she needed her husband and he would need her as they came to grips with the reality that their youngest child was gone. She closed her eyes and asked God to help them both make it through this day.

She used the house phone to call the only person she knew who could help her right now. Cathy was not only her sister-law but also her best friend for more than thirty-five years. Alice stammered, trying to get out the words, but all she could say was, "Todd's dead." No other words were needed. Cathy would come immediately, calling her brother, Chuck, on her way.

Alice hung up the phone and turned to Ben. There were no words they could say to each other that would make this day anything but the nightmare that it was. She leaned into him, feeling his arms wrap around her. They held each other tightly for a few moments, sensing that if one should fall, the other would as well. They did not cry. There was nothing to be said. Neither one of them could answer the question, "Why?"

The doorbell rang.

Alice peeked through the side window of the door. Two detectives, one male and one female, stood on the porch, looking around. The medic who had spoken to Alice earlier came down the stairs and handed her a business card.

"We called them because it's an unknown cause. If you have any questions, don't hesitate to call."

Alice opened the door and moved as the detectives stepped inside. She listened as they introduced themselves as Detectives Matthews and Hatchett. They asked to see the scene. Alice led them upstairs and into her son's room, standing at the door. The female, Hatchett, took out a black pad and looked carefully around the room, taking notes. Matthews roped off the doorway with yellow tape. Alice watched them walking around her son's room, emptiness swelling inside her.

Detective Hatchett looked down at Todd, shaking her head.

"I'm getting so tired of this," she said, bluntly.

Alice looked at her, eyes wide.

"Tired of what?" she asked. The detective pretended not to hear. "Tired of *what?*" Alice insisted, stepping into the room.

"Tired of these young people doing it just 'one more time'."

The detective looked more agitated than angry. Alice saw the sadness in her eyes.

"I don't think so," Alice snapped, her face flushed. "He never used drugs, and he hasn't had a drink for weeks. He wasn't drinking. I would have known. I gave him CPR. I would have smelled it."

Alice felt someone take her elbow and gently guide her from the room.

"We can talk downstairs, " said Dectective Matthews as he led her down the stairs, through the kitchen and into the family room. She sat on the wide recliner and he sat next to her on the couch.

He quietly questioned Alice about the last few days of her son's life. While she spoke, the detective took notes.

Alice explained that, just yesterday, Todd had gone to the doctor for a check-up because he was feeling agitated in the evenings. Even though he was healthy and very physically active, he was also working two jobs. The doctor had examined him thoroughly, especially his heart.

She told the detective Todd was content last night. He was proud that he had saved money to buy his own car. He was ready to drive again. They had picked up Taco Bell for dinner, his favorite fast food. He had tended to her virtual garden on Farmville. They played Family Feud on the computer. He was happy. He was looking forward to his day off. If there had been anything wrong, she would have known. He would have told her.

The doorbell rang again and Cathy came into the kitchen.

"Alice," Cathy said, already crying. Alice went to her, choking back tears as she explained, in a monotone voice, how she found Todd. She laid her head on Cathy's shoulder, and they held each other tightly. Alice held in her tears, gathering strength from the tears of her best friend.

They both turned as the doorbell rang again and she saw the team from the medical examiner's office walk up the sidewalk with their gear. Everything was slowing down. Alice felt as if she were moving through deep, intesifying waves. She took a business card from the detective as he and his partner stepped out the door.

"This is considered an 'unknown death,'" he explained. "The autopsy will be done today. I'll call you as soon as they find out anything. Especially, you know…" He glanced sideways at his partner. "Anything."

As she took the card, she looked up to see her oldest son, Adam, coming down the driveway, trying his best to ignore all the commotion outside. His wife, Lindsay, was by his side. He walked solemnly up the steps and into the house.

Alice reached up to hold him and saw the tenderness of disbelief in his eyes. She held him tightly. They were both too numb to cry. She pulled Lindsay into their embrace, and felt Ben's arms as he invited Cathy to join their sad circle.

They stood there, a wave of immense shock and grief overwhelming them. In the comfort of their embrace, her thoughts railed against her heart.

 Alice felt nothing. A vacuum of darkness had just seized her heart. Her youngest son was dead. Her world as she knew it was no longer. A large piece of her life was instantly gone forever. She blinked back the tears as the emptiness in her heart threatened to shut down her mind.

She pulled away from the embrace, and everyone followed her lead. As they walked into the kitchen, a palpable sadness overwhelmed the room. Cathy moved to make coffee, dumping out the pot of liquid that had cooled through the morning.

As the coroner's team took Todd's body, Alice asked if she could see him one last time. An M.E touched her arm and said," You don't want to see him like this."

Alice leaned against the door to close it. She let out a long sigh, blinking back her tears.

She felt dead inside.

"Mom, it's already on Facebook," Adam said, glancing at his cell phone. "Jeez, how did it get out so fast?"

Alice looked at her husband, who was leaning against the sink, head down.

"We should tell your parents."

He nodded and as he passed, Alice felt the soft brush of his hand across her back. She watched him go upstairs, head down.

The four of them rode together in silence for the 15-minute ride. Alice insisted they tell Ben's parents in person. This was not something to be communicated in a phone call. She remembered when her father had died in a car accident over thirty years ago. It was the immediate family, at her mother's suggestion, who drove over an hour to tell two elderly parents that their son had just died in a car accident.

Alice remembered her own confusion, being young with no children. She couldn't understand their grief when her own mother had just lost *her* husband. Her grandfather was in his room, and it was the first time she heard such sounds coming from anyone. His high-pitched keening was the epitome of the anguish of loss. She had heard it in movies, but never in real life. The sounds filled the entire house that night. She hoped she'd never hear such a sad, forlorn sound again. She chided herself for not understanding then about the love between a parent and a child. With the birth of her first child, Adam, she finally understood. To lose a child was to lose a part of everything that made one complete.

Alice was the one who told Ben's parents. Her words came out simple and direct, with a calmness that surprised her. Todd had died during the night. No one knew why. They would find out later today.

Their reaction and the graciousness with which they accepted the news helped Alice cope with her own pain. They could understand her sorrow. Alice loved her in-laws and knew in her heart that their true grief would be expressed once everyone left.

By the time they returned home, she was exhausted. Her brother had brought several footlong subs and assorted cutlery, and Cathy was busy arranging the table. Lindsay set out glasses and sodas. The landline and cell phones rang or chirped with texts. No one answered. Alice tried to listen to the words of comfort being left, but their messages hurt even more. She turned down the volume for now. She could listen later at the words being said.

She moved to the kitchen and shook her head as her brother offered her a piece of an Italian sub. She was not hungry. At the moment, she felt she would never be able to eat again.

Slowly, she started up the stairs. Soft footsteps behind her told her Adam had followed. From the living room, she heard Ben apologizing to someone for pouring another drink. She heard her brother's quiet words, and she heard Ben begin to sob. She didn't care right now that he was drinking. It just didn't matter. Her heart was breaking and so was his. She wanted a drink with all her heart. Yet she knew it wasn't to drown out the pain. Deep inside, she didn't want to be here right now. Anymore. Ever.

Adam reached to swipe away the yellow tape and they both went into the room. Alice stood at the end of the bed, looking down at the spot near the window where she last saw Todd. Her words trailed off as the memories of that morning flickered quietly. Was it still the same day? Did this all just happen this morning?

"Todd....," she whispered. She sat on the edge of the bed and laid back into the soft impression that he had left on the blanket.

"I can still feel him...." She whispered, breathing in deeply.

"Yeah," Adam agreed as he slumped softly onto the bed beside her. He reached over and put his arm around her to comfort her. She leaned into him and together, mother and brother, held each other, their sadness mingling on the blanket below.

"What happened?" Adam turned to her.

"I came in to wake him up to go to the movies," she whispered. She looked up at the ceiling as tears streamed down her cheeks. "He was just lying here. He was so still," her voice was quiet. " But when I held him, he gurgled. I thought he might still be alive. I mean, he gurgled...."

Her voice trailed softly, and she sniffed back her tears. She turned to Adam and reached over to gently touch his cheek.

"We're going to be alright." The words sounded hollow and she tried to mean them. As if on cue they both sat up, gathered their thoughts, and hugged each other one last time.

The doorbell rang and Alice stood, moving towards Todd's bedroom door. Adam stayed on the bed, saying he'd join her in a minute. She nodded and her sad smile told him she understood.

Todd and Adam were three years apart, and they were very close. Adam both teased and protected his younger brother. Todd would get angry at his teasing, but he looked up to Adam, wanting to be so much like him. As Alice went downstairs to join the others, her heart filled with the love and the loss she felt from Adam. He needed to feel and be near his brother one last time. Alone.

Just the whisper of Todd and his memories.

CHAPTER 4

PEARLS

Todd felt himself being pulled upward, and he watched as his bedroom faded in the soft mist of the clouds. His heart ached with a bewildering sadness--he yearned to stay longer. Anger overwhelmed the sadness as he looked around him.

"No! Not now! Things are just getting good! I'm not ready!" he cried out. Then, as an afterthought: "I was even going to church!"

He heard kind laughter as he earnestly said the words. He strained to see his house, and as the mist parted, he spotted it from his rising distance. It was as though he was looking through a huge telescope. Tears threatened to fall and he squeezed his eyes tight as he tried to ignore the soft voices surrounding him. Gentle arms caressed him as he rose higher and higher through the clouds.

We know, whispered the voices. It was never about church or anything else. We understand. He knew you never left Him. HE gave you three more years-so many prayers were answered then. You healed. You were happy. But now it is time.

Todd allowed himself to drift above the thread of clouds. They parted, and suddenly the sky was filled with a radiant, shining light. He looked around and saw nothing but brightness and soft waves of white. Todd saw a man in a white robe, floating on a hill of bulging softness, beckoning Todd with a white feather pen. He heard someone call out his name.

Todd blinked back a smile. *This is all just a dream,* he thought. *Did that man actually look like Bill Murray?*

Suddenly, he felt a dainty hand slip into his and a quiet voice asked, "Is that your mommy?"

Todd looked down and saw a little girl, around six years old, with pearl-white curls pulled back high with a pink polka-dot bow. She was peeking through the clouds down at the earth below. He realized she was speaking about his mother, who had walked down the hall outside his bedroom and was now resting against the hallway wall.

"Yes, it is," he said.

"Why is she crying?"

"She misses me, I guess."

The little girl looked up at his face, her bright blue eyes questioning, eyebrows knitted together.

"Why are you crying?"

"I miss her."

The little girl crossed her arms and looked at Todd with a sad pout.

"I miss my dog, Shelby."

Todd glanced at her polka dot bow, a smile creeping through his sadness.

"What's your name?" he asked, quietly

"Haley Margaret Jenson," she stated proudly. "What's your name, Mister?" she asked.

He waited a moment before answering, preoccupied with the scene unfolding below them.

"Todd," he said. "Todd Clifford Thomas."

"What do they call you? I have a little friend down there. His name is Brady. I watch over him sometimes when he is sad. His parakeet died."

Todd smiled weakly. *Does she understand where she is?*

"Of course, silly. I'm in Heaven!"

He shrugged, unsurprised that she could read his mind. He glanced again at his surroundings, noticing that he was standing in the middle of billowing cotton candy clouds.

"My dad and brother call me Toddo. My mom just calls me Todd." A pang ran through his stomach as he remembered where he was. They were sitting on a wall of clouds, watching as family arrived below.

Haley nodded her head, her white curls bouncing as she leaned forward to get a better look. She saw a man sitting in an easy chair, looking around at the people surrounding him. He stood up to accept hugs.

"Is that your daddy?"

"Uh-huh."

She turned toward Todd and cupped her hand as if to tell him a secret. He smiled at that, knowing that no one could hear her, anyway. At least no one down there on earth.

"He's drinking, you know." Her eyes were bright with a knowing sadness. He nodded. "He's been drinking since last night."

"I know."

"My daddy and mommy drank all the time." She shook her head, confused. I don't understand how sodas can make you mean." She continued talking, this time out loud.

"I wasn't allowed to drink sodas. Daddy got mad at me one time when I drank his soda. It tasted yucky." She leaned into Todd and whispered, "He threw the glass at me and it broke. It hurt my arm. I started crying and my mommy sent me to my room with no dinner. Just because I cried!" She shrugged.

She'd stated the truth so simply. Todd's face softened as he realized what she had just told him. Her parents had abused her. She slipped her hand inside his again.

"The Scribe told me to come see you," she whispered. They both turned around to see the man with the feather pen standing nearby, his long white robe rippling in the air. Todd noticed he was writing in a large, weathered book. The Scribe waved again, giving them a 'thumbs up' gesture. With eyebrows lifted, Todd nodded back.

A layer of feathery haze drifted around them, changing colors as it did. Todd heard the voices comforting him. His mood was lifted by their words, and although he was unsure what was happening, he was not afraid.

He knew he was in Heaven.

He saw a medic sit by his mother's side, his head down, talking to her. Todd remembered what she had said to him, just yesterday.

She had just picked him up outside the Iron Works, grinning widely as he got into the car. He had smiled at her sheepishly, waiting for her to speak. *She was proud of him. She asked if he remembered what she had told him when he asked if he would ever be in the same place his friends were in life--if he would ever 'catch up' because of his accident.*

Her words echoed in his memory.

"I told you that you needed to make up for those three years from your accident and depression. Remember?" He did." Well," she had continued, "Not only have you 'caught up' to being twenty-six, you're also wise beyond your years." His heart swelled even now as he remembered her words. "And if I were thirty years younger, and, of course, not your mom, I'd think you were hot. Look at you with that hard-working look and all. You're so handsome." The moment she said those words, he had known his world and everything he had regretted from the past was now behind him. He'd grinned at her.

"Mom," he responded, embarrassed--but still, he'd felt pleased.

He grinned now as he had then. Haley squeezed his hand, looking at him with bright eyes.

"She's nice, your mommy. She's funny."

He gave the little girl a nod of acknowledgment.

"Why was she holding you like that? Doesn't she know?"

His voice caught in his throat.

"She's saying good-bye."

They sat there, on the wall of clouds, watching his aunt and uncle, then his brother Adam, and his wife, Lindsay, enter his house below.

His sadness transformed into a subtle aching, a tug of longing. Everything seemed surreal. He willed himself to reach down and try to touch his brother. He wanted to tell him goodbye. He was a funny, smart and protective brother and Todd loved him very much. He wished he had said so more often.

He again felt the anger and resentment. He did not want to be here. He didn't understand why he had gone through everything he had the past few years-the depression, the accident, his recovery from everything-only to have it end when he was finally getting healthy and happy and looking forward to his future.

A firm hand squeezed his shoulder and a deep voice, sounding a bit like his brother, said, "Easy, Todd. You can't change what has happened. It was your time."

Haley rested her head on his arm, her hand soft in his.

He heard her breathing. She must have fallen asleep.

"She needed to sleep. She's been here since yesterday and all she could do was ask what happened." Again, the voice that sounded just like Adam.

Todd squinted up at the man standing next to him. He was a giant of a man, with a barrel chest and familiar, laughing eyes. Todd did not know him--they had never met- yet he recognized him immediately. The soft, golden eyes; the silver-yellow hair glowing in the sunshine, and the voice sounding just like his brother--an older male version of his mother.

"Grandpa Carl?" Todd asked in wonder. The man nodded, folding his large frame to sit down beside his grandson.

"She's going to be all right, you know. She doesn't feel that way now. She's going to miss you for the rest of her life. But she'll be all right."

Todd smiled at the grandfather he had never met.

Grandpa Carl had a kind face, full of joy and laughter, just like his mother had told him and Adam when she recounted stories from her childhood.

Grandpa Carl motioned towards Ben, who was sitting on the couch in the living room, forlorn.

"Your dad's the one who is going to have the roughest time. He's a good man, and he'll get through. But he has choices he needs to make. He can't spend the rest of his life in a bottle." Todd understood the solemn words.

Todd watched his father reach into a paper bag tucked under the recliner and pour some vodka into a glass.

"I think he was drinking last night," Todd said.

"Probably," Grandpa Carl nodded.

"When I asked him if he wanted to go with us to a movie, he said, 'we'll see'."

"Don't we all do that when we're drinking? It's kind of hard to commit to something when you don't know how tomorrow will turn out, right?"

They stood in silence, listening to the quiet sounds from Haley as she slept.

"I don't want to be here," Todd said softly. "I wanted more time. Things were just getting better."

"I know. Same here." They listened to the quiet sounds coming from the little girl as she slept. Todd looked up at him.

"You were in a car accident," Todd said.

"Yep. Wasn't my fault. Didn't expect it. You just never know when it's time." He reached behind his back and brought out a baseball cap. "I've been wanting to give you this since the day you first picked up a bat and ball. I've got one for Adam, too, although I'll have to wait a long time to give him his hat."

The baseball hat Grandpa Carl had in his hand was black and white, with "Washington Senators" scrawled across the front. He placed the cap on Todd's head.

"How old were you, about three?" Grandpa Carl asked.

Todd nodded, thinking about how much he begged his father to play with him and Adam as they tossed the baseball around in the yard. His father agreed, and gave Todd an oversized glove. His father and brother had each taken turns tossing the ball to him. After a while, his mom had joined them. So began his love for the game of baseball.

Todd took off the cap and folded its brim before putting it back on. Haley snuggled into his arm as she hummed in her sleep. Grandpa Carl had moved to his other side, a strong arm draped around his shoulder.

For the first time, Todd felt a sense of belonging.

He watched the people he loved moving about below. He hoped it would not take too long for him to learn how to help them heal. He wanted to make things better for them. As his mother used to tell him, *she* was happy when her family was happy.

He felt relief knowing that if his family were happy down there, he could be happy up here.

CHAPTER 5

GRIEF AND A HARD CHOICE

H er family arrived throughout the afternoon. Everything was
said, and nothing was said. There were no answers. She and
Ben were waiting to hear from the detective, who had promised
to call as soon as the autopsy was performed. Detective Matthews,
she explained, told her because Todd's death was considered "unknown", the autopsy would be performed today, and he would
know something by early evening.

When the phone rang, Alice was ready. She immediately picked
up the receiver and walked into the dining room, closing the double French doors behind her. Detective Matthews asked her several
questions and she answered in short words. She thanked him and
hung up the phone. Sitting in the dining room chair, she cradled
her head in her arms, thinking about what she had just been told.
She was stunned, confused, and extremely relieved the he hadn't
suffered at all.

Alice took a deep breath, gathering her thoughts before opening the doors and slowly walked towards the family room, where
her family waited for an explanation of the incomprehensible. She
glanced up at the cupboard where they used to keep the alcohol as
she made her way down the hallway. No liquor here. Hadn't been

for almost five years. She closed her eyes to shut out the impulse for the one thing she knew would take away the pain and make her feel numb. Rum and Coke. More Rum than Coke. *Not now. Not yet.*

She rested her hands on the railing that separated the kitchen from the living room, with a composure that surprised her.

"That was Detective Matthews. It was his heart," she said, relief flowing through her. "No alcohol, no drugs. They found something in his heart. His heart just stopped."

The room remained quiet as everyone absorbed the information that Todd had passed in his sleep. No pain, no heart attack. His heart just stopped. As far as he knew, he just went to sleep. They call it Sudden Cardiac Death. His was caused by an undetected heart condition that had been slowly damaging his heart for years.

Alice moved through the room, speaking with each person. She felt undeniably calm knowing that Todd had simply fallen asleep. He worked so hard to get better. He'd been going to the gym when he wasn't working. His restlessness, the anxiety before sleeping, the agitation; all along it was his heart. It was damaged so much that his death would have just been be a matter of time.

Late afternoon turned into night and family slowly prepared to leave. Alice walked each family member to the door. Someone mentioned the toad. It wasn't in its usual spot on the corner of the brick porch.

The small, craggy brown toad was special to this family. It had first showed up on the corner of the front step the night Alice's mother had passed away four years ago. Alice had just left the hospital. Before she left that night, she'd sat next to her mother on the hospital bed, took her hand, and leaned towards her, looking directly into her eyes.

"I'll see you tomorrow," she told the woman who had taught her everything about responsibility, courage, forgiveness, and unconditional love. "But just in case..." she took her mother's hand, mustering the strength to continue. "I am who I am because of you. You are the best mother in the world. I love you." Alice had kissed her mom on the lips and heard her whisper back, "I love you."

When Alice came home that night, she almost stepped on the little toad, but it didn't jump or move. It just sat on the corner, like a centaur guarding a valuable treasure. Alice had knelt down and patted it to see if it was alive or had frozen there. It was warm, and bumpy, and still did not move. Throughout the years, they would notice the toad after times of sadness, or happiness. Alice wasn't sure if it was the same toad over the years, but it always seemed around the same size. It was an unspoken promise that no one would try to pick it up. She had no idea where it went when it wasn't here on the steps. It always appeared at night, and was gone by the morning. Since it mostly appeared for Todd, after a while, everyone referred to it as "Todd's Toad." It became part of the family.

"Maybe he went with Todd," someone said, bringing her back to the present.

Alice swallowed. She could not handle the toad going as well.

After the last of family members had left, Alice shut the door behind them and turned to Adam, Lindsay, Cathy and and her brother.

"Can you stay just a little bit longer? I know it's late, but I really don't want to be alone right now."

They joined her as she walked back into the family room, and Alice sighed upon hearing a loud grunt. Ben had passed out in his favorite recliner, arms crossed, his face turned away in despair. She wanted them to stay so she wouldn't drink. She knew there was alcohol hidden around the house. Vodka did not appeal to her. She had almost five years of sobriety; if she were going to blow away all of that time and effort, it would NOT be a random, desperate act. She would get exactly what she had given years ago. She would have a Bacardi and coke and go out with a bang.

She knew that if she took a drink now, she would never stop. "I told him he should sober up or we'll go without him tomorrow," Adam said, nodding towards his father, referring to the funeral home where they had an appointment early the next day. His face reflected the pain it caused him to tell his father that. Alice looked at Adam, and, blinking back tears, nodded.

They spent the next hour talking, smiling, absorbing, remembering. Alice glanced at the DVR clock and saw that it was nearly eleven o'clock. She asked her brother and Cathy if they would join them tomorrow to help with the funeral arrangements. He embraced her firmly and nodded.

She turned to Cathy, and they held each other for a long time. Alice met her sister-in-law for the first time over thirty-five years ago, when her brother started dating her in college. The years had brought them together as sisters, and they became the best of friends. Alice watched them walk down the sidewalk and sighed deeply as she closed the door.

"Let's write the obituary now. You may not feel like it tomorrow," Lindsay suggested.

Alice nodded, and together, she and her daughter-in-law sat down and wrote a simple, beautiful memoir of her son. Lindsay would place it in the newspapers in the morning. With an overwhelming feeling of gratitude, Alice hugged the young lady who brought happiness and comfort to her eldest child. She was overwhelmed with appreciation that Lindsay had calmly guided her through the wording of the piece.

As Adam and Lindsay prepared to leave, just before midnight, Alice's addiction swelled through her. She really wanted a drink right now, but not just to quiet her tortured thoughts. The vast feeling of emptiness bubbled to the surface of her mind. She could not face a day, or even envision a future, without her son.

She wanted to get completely wasted in the comfort of her bathtub, filling up with water. She wanted final oblivion.

She wanted to die.

But it was almost midnight and thankfully the ABC store was closed. They had stopped having alcohol in the house when she had stopped drinking. Ben had tried to stop off and on throughout the past few years, but he always had a stash of Vodka or a four pack of wine hidden somewhere. He respected her efforts, trying not to be so open with his drinking.

Alice sighed as she followed Adam and Lindsay to the front door. It was too late now to even think about drinking, she thought logically. There was too much to do and she knew, without a doubt, that no matter what she drank, or how much she drank, the stark reality would be the same-Todd was gone. Disappearing from this heartbreak would not change a thing. Except she would be miserable and disappointed tomorrow. She couldn't let Adam down. She couldn't let herself down, either.

"Mama Dukes...!" Adam said, gently.

Snapping back from those dire thoughts, she looked at Adam, and she knew right then that she would not die. She could not die. Even though her mind yearned to join Todd, her heart remained here. She had to stay for Adam.

For what would it say to Adam, if she could not live without his brother? She committed to getting through the next few days without drinking. She could do it. She would do it. She had to.

"I'm okay," she told him as he opened the front door.

"No doubt," Adam said, as he hugged her tightly.

As he started to step outside, he stopped quickly, looking down at the doorstop.

"Oh God, Mom--look."

Adam pointed to the brown toad below, which had placed itself in the center of the doorstop, facing the driveway as if to say, *No more harm will come to this house tonight. Not on my watch.*

Adam took a snapshot of the little brown creature, the light from the lamppost casting a halo behind it. As Alice watched them walk down the driveway, she felt new strength. The fact that a little creature could bring out that feeling was extraordinary and she knew without a doubt that somehow, they would get through this horrible nightmare. Alice watched as the SUV moved up the street until it disappeared around the corner. She checked on Ben, snoring loudly, sleeping deeply, covered with the National's Blanket that was given to Todd by his brother just this past summer for his twenty-sixth birthday. She set a glass of ice water on the end table next to him. She did not wake him. He needed the comfort that sleep would bring and she wanted to be alone in her own grief. She tucked the blanket around him and went upstairs.

Someone had closed the door to Todd's room. She opened it, finally feeling an emotion other than sadness for the first time that day. She was angry that someone had closed the door. She leaned against the doorway, looking at the place where, just the evening before, she had spent time with her son.

She imagined him lying there now, deep in sleep. Then, the memory of this morning flashed, and, at last, she allowed herself to lay on his bed and cry. Her tears soaked his pillow as she grabbed it to her, smelling the last remnants of who he was. She tried to keep her cries quiet but they rolled out in sobs as her heart finally gave in to the reality of what was now. She cried until she was too exhausted to cry any more.

She stood and walked numbly to the shower. The tears that flowed this time were washed away by the water. Her body begged for sleep, and she knew that she had to at least lie down.

She went through her usual nighttime ritual without thinking. She had one thing on her mind: she did **not** want to drink. She would not listen to the voice whispering in her ear, *you know what will make you feel much better. You know how to make everything just go away.*

She knew what she had to do.

She set the alarm for 7:05am, and selected the clothes she would wear in the morning. She needed a meeting to keep her balanced.

She climbed into bed wearing one of Todd's favorite long-sleeved shirts, turned on the TV, and leaned back against the pillows.

She felt nothing at all. She reached next to her for the Hallmark pillow Todd had given her for Mother's Day just last year. It read, *"A mother's heart is a wonderful place where her children always have a home."*

Alice buried herself deep beneath the covers, holding her pillow tightly. She wanted to go through the events of this day, over and over. She wanted to make the moment of finding Todd, the snapshot in her mind of seeing him, so real that when she woke up, she would not have to remember. She learned that when her father died; she did it again when her mother passed. She had to do it now.

Instinct more than anything else tugged at her memory, and she went through the day, from the time she woke up and found Todd, until this moment right now. She needed to process everything. She wanted to remember when she woke up, that her life had changed completely and forever.

She needed to rest. She drifted into a dreamless sleep, listening to the soft sounds of the television. When the alarm chirped several hours later, she opened her eyes and remembered. There was great sadness, but not the extreme shock of realizing that her son was no longer here.

She stared at the ceiling until the tears that threatened to fall simply dried without dropping. Her heart felt heavy but she knew she had to get up. Something deep inside her told her she HAD to get through this day. Somehow.

Being in a meeting, absorbing the comfort of other humans that struggled with their alcoholism, would give her emotional sustenance to face the second worst day of her life.

CHAPTER 6
STORY, STORIES

Todd turned away from the events on Earth. He was alone now. He looked around at the little ones drifting softly among the clouds as nighttime slowly deepened below. He saw Grandpa Carl standing on a carpet of lush green grass, playing catch with a group of angels. Music and laughter filled the air. When the clouds drifted apart, he could see two wooden structures, high on stilts, neon lights flashing a message on the roof *'Come join us!'* People were standing and talking to each other. There were balloons and streamers and the bass of the music pulsated all around. This was a celebration.

Todd looked behind him, and saw another structure made of golden timber. The blue peak of the roof slanted down to meet the sides of the building, and one large window flanked the entire front from corner to corner.

He was suddenly aware that everything had stopped.

Silence.

Todd looked back down the hill. Grandpa Carl stood in the center of a cluster of older angels, looking outwards towards a wave of clouds that crested gently downward towards them. The people in both houses below him had turned to face the horizon.

A myriad of colors gradually creeped up and spread across the sky, like fingers coiling ribbons. First red, then orange, then yellow, until the sky was filled with a variety of glorious hues that blinded those watching with their brilliance.

Sunrise had broken and it was a brand-new day.

"Toddo!"

Todd looked at his Grandpa, and quickly caught the ball he tossed with his left hand.

"There's nothing like that!" his grandfather said. Todd nodded and lobbed the ball back.

Up here, time was elusive, and the only way Todd could mark each passing day was by the colorful trees surrounding his house below, which became bright against the backdrop of the morning sky. The Japanese maple that stood along the driveway was in full crimson feathers.

Everything seemed so surreal. He felt fine. He felt alive. He felt that this was all a dream.

Suddenly a thought came to him. He remembered Grandpa Carl saying that one day he would learn how to help the ones he loved. He closed his eyes and concentrated, willing himself to be back on Earth. He wasn't sure how any of this worked, but he would try.

When he opened his eyes, he was in his parents' bedroom. His father was snoring in peaceful slumber. His mother was curled up, facing away from him, holding the pillow Todd had given her last year.

She mumbled something in her sleep and her hand reached out towards him. Tissues sprawled along the carpet, and he bent down to reach for her hand.

He felt the warmth of her skin. A tear began to fall from her closed eyes.

"I miss you, Todd," she whispered.

In that instant, he was yanked back up into the clouds. It happened so quickly that it took a few moments for his thinking to catch up. He sensed a hand on his shoulder and he turned to see The Scribe, the man who welcomed everyone into Heaven.

"Oh, that's a big No-No," The Scribe said, and opened his huge white book, pretending to write something down. "That's one strike against you." He held back a little smile as he tried to frown.

"What did I do wrong? "

"You visited your loved ones. You can't do that yet."

"You're actually going to give me a strike? Isn't this Heaven?"

The Scribe stood there, touching the white feather pen repeatedly against his lips.

"No, buddy, it's Iowa," he quipped. "Of course, it's Heaven! It would be a totally different experience if it were somewhere else." He leaned closer, winking. "If ya know what I mean."

"How come we get strikes?"

Todd was totally confused. How can such a wonderful place like Heaven be giving out strikes to someone who doesn't even know what the rules are?

The Scribe rolled his eyes and dropped the book to his side.

"I'm kidding! There's 'no crying in baseball' and there are no strikes in Heaven! Geez..." His smile softened the words he spoke. "You are a bit naïve," he squinted an eye. "Smart, handsome and funny, but..."

The Scribe hefted the book into his arms and started skimming through pages, making clicking sounds with his tongue.

"Ah, here you are." He started reading quickly down the page, every now and then making small noises of approval or curiosity as he reviewed Todd's life.

"Hmmm, you've been a good kid all your life it seems...except," he glanced over his reading glasses at Todd. "Except for the DUIs. What *were* you thinking?"

Todd made a sound." Not much. Thought I could drive."

The Scribe tried to feign scorn, but he said, "Yeah, right. That's what they all say."

"Look, you're a good kid," he continued. "Seems to me like you had a good life and that everything that happened was maybe because of bad choices."

Todd nodded.

"Yeah, I know," The Scribe said, with regret. "You were on so much medication from that doctor you were seeing that you actually *thought* you were okay to drive."

The Scribe closed the book, flipping down the corner of the page so that he could easily find it again "You remember when you called your mom to come up to the bar and sing karaoke with you that night?" he asked.

Todd nodded.

"She really wanted to join you. She even took a shower to see if she could get energized since they just got back into town. Remember what she asked you?"

Todd nodded again, trying to pay attention. "Yeah, she asked me if I had been drinking....and I said no. I just felt really happy."

Todd prepared himself for the lecture that would come, but The Scribe only looked him straight in the eyes.

"She was so thankful you were happy, and she believed you weren't drinking. That's why she didn't come. She thought you were finally happy. She wanted to give you your space to be happy."

"I lied to her," Todd admitted, sadly.

"Oh, yeah, that. Don't worry. She wasn't mad at you. But after your accident, *she* felt so guilty that she had believed you. *She* felt if she had come up there and sung Karaoke with you, that you would have made it home safely. *She* felt your accident was her fault."

"I know. She apologized for that."

"Well, I want to tell you something. Everything happened the way it was supposed to. If your mother had come up to the bar that night and driven you home, another car would have gone over the middle lane and headed right into your car. That driver would have died, and both you and your mom would have been seriously injured. You would have survived." With a kindness in both his eyes and voice, The Scribe continued gently, "But your mom would have died."

Todd looked at him, speechless. Tears threatened to spill from the corners of his eyes.

The Scribe rested the book against his chest. "If she had joined you, by the time you decided to leave, that other driver would have already been on Old Bridge Road. You would have collided. It would have changed everything. So many lives. *Everything.*"

"Because of your accident, that driver saw the commotion ahead and pulled off onto a side street to sleep it off. Two lives were saved because your mom stayed home. Look at you. It wasn't your time either because of your little 'white lie,' that man made it home to his pregnant wife and three children."

Todd lowered his head, taking in all that was said.

"She's a good one, that mother of yours." The Scribe nudged him, gently.

"Yeah, I know."

"Too bad I'm up here and she's down there..." The Scribe said with a sly grin. "Look, I'm kidding! Todd, lighten up a bit. This is Heaven. We like to have fun. Some of us have more fun up here than we *ever* did down there."

Todd sat on a wall of clouds, his elbows resting on his knees, watching the world below begin a new day. He looked at the out-stretched hand of the older angel.

"Here's the deal. I'm The Scribe, but some people call me Scribs." His eyes sparkled as he spoke. "I keep track of everyone who comes up here. Many of them stay and become Elders. They escort the Newbies. They make sure no one feels pain."

He glanced over at Todd, raising his eyebrows.

"You didn't feel any pain, did you?"

"No," Todd spoke slowly. "I think I just fell asleep."

"Good. That's the way it's supposed to be. Most of the children up here have come to us through circumstances that could not be stopped. They experienced joy and love until the moment they came up here. They left behind families that will always miss them. They are all on the other side of that hill; they are waiting to be reborn."

Todd watched as Scribs removed his glasses and wiped his eyes with the back of his sleeve.

"Not all the children are lucky. Some of them had truly bad situations on earth. Humans with free will...."

Todd looked around him as a gentle breeze gently rocked billowy beds with waking angels yawning sweetly.

"How are you doing? Feeling okay about all of this?" The Scribe raised an eyebrow.

Todd shrugged and smiled, sadly. "I really don't have a choice, do I?"

Scribs leaned on the wall by his side, shaking his head, watching the world below. "Good. You have a job to do. Your heart was failing, and it was only a matter of time. There are many children who are here only because those who called themselves 'parents' or 'caregivers' weren't that at all. Your job is to show all these little ones *your* family. Show them your brother, your friends, their families. Show them that not all parents are bad. They need to see that most parents, like your mom and dad, would do anything to protect their children. Anything."

Scribs pointed a silver remote control at the sky. A large theatre screen blanketed the expanse. Figures flashed on the screen. Todd recognized the scene immediately.

It was the summer of his junior year in high school, and the temperature was well over one hundred degrees. Todd had overheated while pitching a game, and was throwing up blood in the dugout. Someone told his mother, and she went to him immediately. She soaked a towel with cool water and placed it on the back of his neck. While a player held the towel on the nape of Todd's neck, she ran up the gravel hill to get her car.

Within moments, she had driven her brand-new Mercedes down to the ballfield, and another parent helped Todd into the air-conditioned car. She had called 911, and they told her that she could get him to the hospital into the cooled environment of her car before rescue could reach the field. Not once had she worried about her car. Her only instinct was to get him cooled off. She had called ahead to the emergency room, and they were waiting for him when she pulled up. She stayed by his side the entire time.

Other scenes flashed overhead; holidays, birthdays, field trips, regular days. Todd watched as his family gathered to celebrate each day with friends and other family members.

"Look," The Scribe said, indicating all around them. A group of little children, still sleepy from their rest, were beginning to gather, watching the sky screen in awe as they saw something few had seen in their time on earth: happy families.

The Scribe turned to Todd with gentle eyes.

"You can help them heal. It will help you accept your situation, as well. You had an amazing life, Todd. Tell them about it. Show them that parents can be good people. Give them hope. Especially Haley, who came a few hours before you did. She's been sad and troubled because she can't understand why her stepmom would hurt her so much, but even worse, why her daddy didn't help her at all. She has no closure. They haven't found her body. Not yet, maybe not ever."

As Todd looked around at all the little children, he felt a small hand slip into his. He looked down at Haley, whose face was bright with eager anticipation. She leaned her head against his arm, and started humming.

" I love you, Todd," she said, with the innocence of a child.

The older angel cleared his throat.

"You will have your grandpa Carl, your Meme and many others, who will help you along the way. In time, you will be able to visit Earth. Your mom feels you every day. You can let her know from here that you are all right."

"But what do I tell them?"

"Anything and everything. Even the times when you got in trouble. They need to see that parents can discipline without hitting. Parents can love without hurting."

With a sigh, The Scribe turned to walk away, book under his arm, feather pen stuck behind his ear. As he walked by Haley, he gently ruffled her curls. She giggled, and ducked her head towards Todd.

"Don't worry about your dad, either," he called over his shoulder. "He needs to work through things in his own way. The drink is the only way he knows how to deal with losing you right now. He's never lost anyone so close to his heart. Give him time. He'll get it. Most usually do. In the meantime, pray for him. Any time is a good time to pray."

CHAPTER 7

COPING

Losing a child is the worst thing that could happen to any parent. Alice realized that only when she became a mother herself. When her father had died suddenly, she had spent the night with her grandparents, not understanding their grief because she only saw his loss through her own eyes and that of her mother. She had never heard keening before, but the desperate sounds that vibrated throughout the solemn night from her grandfather's room struck her through her heart.

She didn't sleep much that night, wanting to comfort her Pop, yet not fully grasping the magnitude of his loss. She would quietly open the door, and sit on the edge of her grandfather's bed, patting his back, stroking his cheek. He would eventually fall silent from his tears, and a soothing hum would come from him as he fell into a wounded sleep.

It seemed that night lasted forever until she heard her grandmother wake, wash her face in the bathroom, and go into the kitchen to put on a pot of coffee. It was almost 5 am.

When she had Adam, Alice finally understood their grief. When Todd was born, she knew her life was complete. Only then, did she begin to understand the power of the devastation of losing one's child. She prayed it would never happen to her children.

Now she knew. Now she felt. Now she lived the understanding.

She felt the loss in every part of her body from the moment she woke up until, exhausted, her mind craved the sleep she needed. Sleep brought relief to the agony of every single breath. She wished she could hold him one last time.

Just a week ago, she had a dream that made absolutely no sense at all. She was in the house where she grew up, in her old bedroom. She was a teenager. Purple colors reflected off the walls and a gentle breeze danced across the lacy curtains. She was looking through a box of photos that she found while cleaning the junk from under her bed. As she sat on the bed, looking at the pictures, she heard a familiar voice call from the kitchen.

"Mama Dukes!" She recognized the voice of Adam and it all seemed so natural. What she heard next was familiar as well.

"Hey, Mom. I'm here."

Even in her dream, she knew it could not be real. Todd walked down the hall to her bedroom, looking healthy and happy, with a wide grin spreading through the trimmed beard he always wore. But it felt real.

In the dream, he stopped in the doorway. Standing, the box of photos scattered along the floor. She went to him and took him in her arms. She hugged him and he hugged back. He took one of her hands and stepped away, smiling.

She cried. He was not gone. He was here.

Her real tears woke her up, and she squeezed Ben's hand that she was holding. She opened her eyes and realized his hand was no longer holding hers. She turned to kiss Ben on the cheek, but he was snoring loudly from the other side of the bed. His back was to her, sleeping soundly.

Then she knew.

Her heart swelled as she realized that part of the dream was real. That somehow, Todd had reached through her dream to hold her hand and touch her. She nestled into her pillow, tucking the hand beside her cheek, and before she fell asleep she whispered, "I miss you so much."

Time was marked at first by days, then by Fridays. Fridays gave way to another week and then measured by the twenty-fourth of each month. Alice forced herself to relearn a new normal, trying not to isolate. She looked forward to Adam's phone calls in the morning, checking on them, seeing if they were doing all right. Later in the day, she would get a call from Cathy, who would say, "Guess who's here, Aunt Alice?"

This was her signal to Alice that Cathy's grandson was visiting for the day. Alice would finish whatever she was doing and eagerly join them for the rest of the afternoon, filling her heart and mind with a peace that comes with being around a toddler.

She immersed herself doing mindless chores, going to meetings, or helping others until nighttime when she fell onto her bed, exhausted. She cried regularly in the shower, letting the water wash away the deep misery of her loss. Each night she fell asleep on a damp pillow. Kleenex became her best friend.

She would pray.

One thing she knew without a doubt, something she intrinsically must have learned from her mother. Life will go on, with or without her. She had to either catch up to the world, or slowly succumb to her grief. Alice knew she couldn't live in a cocoon, sheltering herself from any pain, even though every part of her body begged to do so. She read somewhere that human nature instills a reset button for everyone. She hoped that one day, she could reset the button against the tremendous pain of today, and embrace the memory of Todd with sweet memories and laughter that, for at least twenty-six years, she had a life that was wonderful.

Slowly, she edged herself back into living, but she was only coping.

Driving behind cars, she now noticed the bumper stickers that showed stick people of a family; usually a mom and dad, children of different ages, an occasional dog or cat stretched along the rear window of a car. Seeing the bumper stickers reminded her that her family was down one loved one. She was ironically grateful she never had a bumper sticker on her car with the four of them. She could never remove any one of them, not that she would.

One day just after Hallowe'en, she finally got up the courage to go into one of her favorite department stores and felt relief as she entered the doors and browsed the new fall clothing line. She looked aimlessly at the shoes and jewelry. Anything. Everything. As she went to the back of the store to look at the linens and towels, she stopped suddenly and swallowed hard.

Christmas was everywhere.

It was the beginning of November. Christmas trees were graced with tinsel and ornaments and the sparkle of the season. Wherever she looked, brought the loss of her son smack in her face.

This Christmas would be without him.

Feeling her heart pumping and her breath slipping away, she turned and immediately retreated to the sanctuary of her car, slammed the door and lowered her head on the steering wheel, sobbing. *Will it ever stop hurting? Ever?*

She would drive home, get in her pajamas and crawl into bed, turning on the TV to keep her company. Ben would be downstairs, eventually getting out of bed only to sit on the recliner in the family room and pretend he was not drinking. Alice knew he was doing that for her. Right now, she did not care. She was just short of five years in her sobriety, and she made it an effort each day to make it to January 29. She would do it for Todd. She would do it for Adam. She would do it for Ben.

Mostly, she would do it for herself. She learned, just as getting into recovery and not drinking, she had to do this for herself. She wanted to be that person who wanted to be better.

Alice worried about Ben. He would wake up every morning, having slept in the comfort of his favorite recliner. He would try to do some chores around the house. By mid-morning he was already drinking, settling back in the recliner, watching Jerry Springer. She would sit with him for a bit in the evening, on the edge of the chair, her arms around his shoulders, her head nestled next to his.

He would talk about Todd and how much he missed him. She would listen, absorbing his memories. He would talk until there was nothing left to say. Ben would apologize while he fixed another drink. The smell of liquor triggered long repressed memories for her of how good a drink would feel right now. The smoothness of the rum would warm her throat, tickling her mind, until final solace came from not feeling anything at all.

But she wouldn't. She couldn't. She would kiss Ben's forehead, holding back the growing resentments that threatened her sobriety. Ben had it lucky. He still had the salve that would ease his breaking heart, of course, until tomorrow.

In these times, she would go to a meeting or go shopping; if her willingness was waning, she would spend the night with her brother and Cathy. She would always return the next day, because no matter how angry and resentful and desperate she was, they needed each other, more now than any other time in their lives.

For her, after all her time and effort, drinking alcohol was no longer an option. It was only a temporary solution against the pain of reality. She couldn't bring Todd back, no matter how much she drank to numb the pain of losing him.

On this brisk December morning, the alarm buzzed at 7:05AM. Alice dropped a leg out from under the covers, reached for the remote to turn on the TV, and waited until her foot began to twitch.

Within minutes, her leg would begin to twitch, then swing. She sighed. Her brain was awake, urging her body to move. Throwing back the covers, she went downstairs, fixed a cup of coffee, went back upstairs, and snuggled in bed. Sipping coffee, she watched her favorite crime shows. Anything else was too depressing. This was the only escape she knew and som ething she understood. Comedies made her cry. She didn't feel like laughing anymore. Current news was disheartening. Sadness enveloped her every thought. Watching her favorite crime shows gave her the inane comfort she desperately wanted right now. Looking out her bedroom window, she could see the cloudless sky through the lingering leaves on the tree branches. Even though it was almost winter, they had yet to have a frost. This was exactly the kind of picturesque day people yearn for. Nothing bad can ever happen on such a wonderful day as this.

But it does. It did just weeks ago.

She thought about her new normal and the well-meaning things people would say to her. No matter where she went, she faced the anxiety of running into an acquaintance or a friend. Those who knew her family would instantly come up, give a hug, and ask how everyone was. She embraced them for the love they gave. Without knowing what to do, they did exactly what was needed.

But there were others, people she knew for a long time. They avoided her, pretending not to see her in the grocery store, or anywhere else. If they did stop to chat, they spoke about mundane things, avoiding the topic completely. Or they would acknowledge her loss, comforting her by saying things they thought would be helpful.

"I don't know how you get out of bed each day. I would want to die." *Didn't they understand that's exactly what she wanted to do?*

"He's in a better place." *Don't you think I know that?*

"I know how you feel. I lost my brother (or mother or cousin or friend) just last year." *Yeah. I get that. But did you really feel the air was sucked out of you with a lightning punch as you lost a part of your heart because it was shattered beyond belief?* Alice tried to reconcile that they were trying to reach out to her with the only part of their lives they connected with.

One friend tried to explain why Ben was having such a hard time getting sober afterwards.

"Well, you know. There's a different bond between a father and his son. He'll get the hang of it. It's just harder on him is all." *For real?*

She would reply, "I had a special bond with my son, too! I knew him long before he took his first breath in this world!"

She remembered what a good friend had said to her, trying to help her understand that some people didn't know how to handle grief. *Yeah, I get that. So, I have to be the one to understand their awkwardness? I'm tired of understanding things.*

Yet, through all the comments that meant well, it was the ones that came from his friends and family and all who knew Todd best that lifted her heart. Their memories of how good and kind Todd was; his humor and how he judged no one. If someone was his friend, they were his friend for life. Especially soothing, were when several of them said to her that when things in their life that were difficult, at a crossroad of decisions, they would often ask, "*What would Todd do?*"

Knowing this, Alice felt deep appreciation for those who truly knew who her son was. When they had the viewing, and Todd was dressed in his Number 38 National's jersey instead of some over-dressed suit and tie, there was a comfort in the room. This was Todd. This was who he was. He went by his own set of rules-a non-conformist who gently fit in with societies rules, when he had to. These were the comments she fell asleep with.

There was only one time when Alice decided she would ask God to take her from this pain. She had laid on Todd's bed, in her sweatpants and his favorite Nike shirt, closed her eyes, and prayed.

"God, please just take me now. I'm tired and I hurt and I don't know if I can do this anymore. I think I'd make a really good angel and I could help you up there far better than down here." Tears streamed down her cheeks and she closed her eyes, waiting to fall into a heavenly forever sleep.

She waited, and waited, and waited for the welcoming calm that would free her from this wretched pain. Then her foot began to twitch, her breathing quickened and she realized it just wasn't going to happen. Sighing deeply, she sat up. "Oh, all right. I guess not."

Thinking back on it now, she smiled sadly. Asking God to take her had been a silly thing to do. But then again, when one is overwhelmed with the challenge of living each day without a loved one, silly things could be the only way to make it through each moment.

Alice went into the kitchen as a long, loud yawn came from the family room. She decided that today she would plant the bulbs she bought this past September before her life changed. It was the first of December and they hadn't had an Indian Summer yet so she knew the ground would not be hard.

One year she actually planted bulbs in January, even though everyone told her it was too late. But they came up in late April. She had some little groups of flowers that would gently embrace the ground around the wooden, cast iron bench where Todd had spent so many nights after his accident, thinking about his future and the better choices he wanted to make.

"Want to help me put the bulbs in the ground?" she wistfully asked Ben as he passed by her, heading up the stairs. His eyes were bleary from a night of drinking and a trail of sweat and alcohol left its wake.

"Nah, I want to go to a meeting." She tried not to react. "I've got to get myself together."

She watched him as he rested a hand on the railing.

"I'm meeting with someone today who wants me to come work with him, help him start his company." She looked up at him, saw his sad smile. "I guess retirement is over. I should get back to work."

"It will be good for you," Alice said. "I'm thinking of subbing; maybe after Christmas." She'd already filled out the application and emailed it to the county. But after Todd died, she called the county and said she wasn't ready. She was grateful that they both had retirement investments to allow them to grieve without money worries. She knew she was blessed for that.

Sighing, she shrugged away the heavy feeling that was always a tear away. For Ben, throwing himself into something new was the way he dealt with things he could not handle. He would try again to make it through a day without drinking. Each time, a flutter of hope was tamped with a reminder of the way things usually ended within a day. Alice understood the cycle of alcoholism all too well.

The sun shone brightly as the garage doors rolled up and she blinked as she took a breath of the fresh early December air.

CHAPTER 8

HALEY

Todd found comfort in Heaven. His distress at the suddenness of his death, and his angst over missing life on Earth, was slowly being replaced by a feeling of peace and the finality of acceptance. Contentment increased each day as he shared stories of his time on Earth, appreciating that, except for the year and a half of his depression and accident, he had a happy life.

Little angels floated gently on billowy beds, or sat at his feet, listening as he told story after story about his life, his friends and especially his family. For longer stories, the Sky Screen appeared in the clear sky above and everyone nestled around him, watching with dreamy eyes as funny events played out on the screen, enhancing Todd's stories. There were several episodes the little ones wanted to see over again, and they laughed harder each time, some falling over into the fluffy clouds. Like when his mom laughed so hard she would snort. They all loved that one, making funny snorting noises.

The episode playing now was one of their favorites. It showed a time after Todd's accident when he was working for a company 45 minutes from home. It was the evening shift, and he was still not yet medically cleared to drive. His parents were visiting friends and had planned to pick him up on their way back home. After his shift was over, he walked a mile to a local sports bar, where he listened to a rap band and enjoyed the company of young people he had come to know.

When the restaurant closed around midnight, his parents were still over an hour away. Someone in the band offered to take him home after their next gig in Washington, DC.

Without a second thought, he agreed and texted his parents. He shared a beer in the van and helped them set up at their next event. He was dropped off around four the next morning. He waved goodbye and opened his front door.

His mom was sitting at the top of the stairs, waiting with a smile.

"Hey," he said, smiling sheepishly.

"Hey. So, you got a ride home with a rap group?"

He nodded, grinning.

"You went to DC with them?"

He started up the stairs towards her, still grinning.

"What did you guys do?"

"Hung out. I sang a bit karaoke. It was cool."

She hugged him. "Sorry we were so late," she said. "We won't be late again."

He nodded and smiled. "They said I can get a ride anytime. They just finished early last night."

Haley watched the screen, hands on her face, enchanted.

Todd noticed the happy faces of the little ones as they listened to his stories and felt a sharp pang in his chest as he realized just how much his life had mattered.

Haley leaned against his arm, and looked up at him with bright eyes.

"I really like your mommy." She always spoke in whispers. "I wish I had a mommy like yours."

"Hey, Toddo, I got this." Grandpa Carl had been listening nearby. He called over his shoulder, "Hey, Scribby! When will that ice cream be ready?"

"Will you PLEASE stop calling me Scribby! That's not my name!"

Todd heard the jovial tone in the Elder's voice and turned to his grandfather.

"There's ice cream up here?"

Grandpa Carl adjusted Todd's baseball cap.

"You have no idea how wonderful it is up here. You'll find this place is better than anyone imagined."

Dozens of little wings fluttered eagerly as the angels followed Grandpa Carl. Up and down, all over the sky, happy giggles reverberated as Grandpa Carl and the children crowded around an ice cream truck.

Todd looked down at Haley. Her eyes were glistening as she watched everyone race to get ice cream.

"Don't you want some ice cream?"

She didn't move.

Todd gently nudged her head, and she looked up at him. He nudged her again, and she gently pushed back. She asked if she could sit on his lap. He hoisted her onto his legs and made a pillow of the clouds that wrapped around her. The clouds turned a soft yellow, reflecting her yellow dress.

"What did your mommy give to that lady?"

Todd remembered the last scene on the sky screen, when his mom handed a piece of paper to a friend of hers who had been crying.

"It was the money she won at the casino."

"But why did she give it to her? Your mommy won the money. She should keep it. She could buy clothes and stuff and it would make her feel better."

"Well...the friend that was crying was behind in her rent and her family was being evicted. She had a lot of medical bills that she needed to pay, and she was behind two month's rent. She didn't know where she would get the money."

Haley scrunched up her nose, frowning, trying to understand. "So, your mommy just *gave* her that money?"

"Yeah, she does that sometimes." he said proudly.

"What does she want from that lady?"

Todd shrugged, and smiled again. "Nothing."

He watched as Haley twisted a curl around her finger. She looked up at Todd with soft eyes.

"Why is your mommy so nice?"

Todd shrugged and with a smile said, "That's just her."

"My mommy would never give anything to anyone. One time my neighbor asked for a ride to work because her car was low on gas." Haley crossed her arms and exaggerated a frown. "Mommy told the lady 'no.' She should always keep gas in her car and she shouldn't ask for things if she can't take care of herself." Todd had to agree that Haley's mother wasn't nice at all.

"Well, my mommy never made that sound, either. The one your mommy makes when she laughs really hard." She glanced up at Todd. "Is there something wrong with your mommy 'cause she's nice, and she snorts?"

Todd chuckled loudly, knowing his mom would have laughed at the comment.

"No. That's just her."

"Well, I like that sound she makes." Again, the secret whisper. "My mommy didn't laugh much at all. All she did was yell at me and tell me that I'm dumb and lazy."

She shrugged her shoulders.

"Of course, I'm dumb! I'm only six years old!" she proclaimed honestly. "But I'm not lazy..."

Todd watched her pull a little string from her yellow dress.

"She yelled at daddy all the time, too."

"Didn't she laugh sometimes, like when she was reading to you, or watching TV?"

Her little head shook back and forth as she sighed.

"Nope. She never did that stuff. She didn't even cry when I died." Todd could barely hear her words. "My daddy didn't either."

A soft flash appeared in the clouds as the sky screen appeared.

Todd saw a little girl with white curls and a yellow dress getting off a school bus. He saw someone help her down, and it was then that he noticed she had on a leg brace and special metal crutches. He glanced down at her legs now. Both legs were crossed at the ankle.

"That is Mrs. Tinsel," Haley said. "She's my friend. She's the one who helps me in school. She's nice, too!"

On the screen, Haley waved goodbye to the children on the bus and started up the sidewalk towards a house. A lady was standing in the doorway, her arms crossed, a scowl on her face. She looked too old to have a little girl as young as Haley, he thought. Maybe this lady was her grandmother.

Haley leaned into Todd, reading his thoughts.

"No. That's my mommy. See? She's not smiling. I am always happy to come home after school. I always liked to see my mommy on the porch."

Todd watched in silence as the woman on the porch yelled something to the Haley on the screen. Haley dropped her crutches and started to walk up and down the sidewalk, struggling with every step. Todd cringed, holding back his anger. Haley's mother kept yelling to go faster and strengthen her legs, before she could come in and have her snack. The Haley onscreen almost fell, and reached for her crutches. Todd looked down at Haley, her face transfixed at the scene.

"I'm not lazy," she whispered. "It hurt to walk without my crutches."

Todd looked around for The Scribe and caught the older angel's eye. His eyebrows raised at the question he wanted to ask. Why would they show something so hurtful on the Sky screen? He heard The Scribes voice inside, calming him down. This was nothing new for Haley. She lived this every day. Todd needed to see. He needed to understand.

"Why didn't my mommy like me?"

Silence.

Todd's anger shifted to sadness. There were no words to explain any of that behavior.

Haley exclaimed, "That's my daddy coming home!"

On the sky screen, a man drove up in his truck, hardly noticing Haley walking up and down the street.

"Hi, Daddy!" she called out. Todd's heart ached for the little girl on the Sky Screen as her father ignored her and went into the house. He watched the Haley on the sky screen drop her head and begin to hobble up the sidewalk to the front steps.

They heard loud voices coming from the house as she started to sit, but stood immediately when her father came storming out of the house. He glanced down at his daughter with a melancholy smile and stormed down the walk to grab her crutches. He bent down to Haley, handing her the crutches, saying something Todd could not hear. He stomped back to his pickup truck, backed out of the driveway, and raced down the street.

He never looked back at his daughter.

The screen door opened and her mother stood aside, glaring at the little girl.

"Get in here, now!" She pointed her finger into the house. "Look what you did. You made your daddy angry and he left. No dinner for you, nothing. Get to your room and don't come out until I tell you to!"

The little girl with the white curls stepped up onto the porch, struggling with her crutches. She slowly limped into the house and the screen door slammed shut.

The Sky Screen went dark, and the swirling clouds reappeared. Todd knew that whenever the screen went dark, that somethings should not be seen.

He heard Haley's soft breathing as she rested against his chest. She had fallen asleep.

Todd glanced down at earth, seeking comfort from what he had seen unfold.

His mom was setting a box of bulbs on some mulch beneath the bench where he would sit, thinking, making plans for a better future. Sometimes his mother would join him outside, where she'd sit next to him, arms crossed, legs stretched out. These were moments he always enjoyed. He talked, she listened. Always, she would tell him things would work out well.

Todd was glad she had chosen to plant bulbs beneath that bench. He smiled at what they called her "brown thumb." *These* bulbs would grow where they were. Even if she had to sit out there every night, and tend to them every day. They would grow.

Haley stirred in his arms and as he rested his chin gently on the top of her head, her curls tickling his beard, and he understood how he could help her. He looked over at Grandpa Carl, who nodded at him, grinning.

"Did you watch it?"

Todd nodded.

"There's more," Grandpa Carl sat next to him, gently stroking the top of Haley's curls.

"She didn't get dinner that night. Her mother blamed her for making her dad angry. She did nothing wrong, Todd. This little girl never did anything wrong. She was afraid of her step-mom."

Haley opened her sleepy eyes, looking up at Grandpa Carl. He smiled, encouraging.

"My stubby was really blue and it *hurt really bad* and then I threw up. Mommy was really mad at that." She paused for a moment, but knew she had to tell him what happened. He had to know in order to understand.

"I tried to go to my room, but mommy tripped me and I fell down the basement stairs. I don't think she meant to...but she didn't come down after me." Pause. "I hit my head on the corner and it really, really hurted." Pause. "Then I started to get dizzy and I cried for Daddy, but Mommy said he wasn't home. Then I went to sleep."

Todd held her tightly, pressing his head softly against the top of her curls. He didn't know what to say. The actions were incomprehensible. He noticed a dark look cross over his grandfather's face. Disgust.

"I couldn't keep my eyes open. I heard my daddy but he didn't do anything. I tried to reach up. I just wanted my daddy to hold me because I was starting to get really cold. But he didn't. He was just staring at me and then my eyes closed."

Haley scooted off Todd's lap. The pale, yellow clouds drifted around her, comforting her.

"Daddy got a blanket, and I thought he was going to take me upstairs to my bed and tell me he loved me, but he carried me outside to the back yard."

Haley's teardrops fell to earth in the form of tiny snowflakes.

Todd's face went stone cold. He didn't want her to see the anger and disgust that he was feeling towards the parents he did not know and could never understand. He never felt this anger against any other human being before. His feelings were reflected on the face of his grandfather.

"I started to feel hot...and then..." Haley's voice perked up. "Then I was up here! It didn't hurt anymore! "

Todd forced a smile as he looked at her.

"Well, I guess you were here to welcome me!" His voice melted with kindness when he saw her bright smile.

"I've been up here waiting for you!" she said, eagerly. "Grandpa Carl told me all about you and asked me to help *you* when you got here. And I did!"

Todd nodded and watched as his mother put on his Nike sweatshirt, bringing the collar up to her face. She would often put on a T-shirt or a sweatshirt that he used to wear. He now understood that this kind of love was what parents should be about. When his mother found him that morning, she could have been afraid of what would happen and then throw his body away like garbage, claiming he disappeared or ran away. From the shows he watched while he was alive, he knew this is what some parents did, or even worse, set their child on fire or grind them up in a wood grinder. But his parents immediately called for help. Even though they didn't know yet what had happened,they called to help him. That's what parents *should* do. His heart swelled with the complete understanding that parents who actually *loved their children unconditionally,* would do anything to keep their children safe. Anything. Like call 911.

"Haley, there's Todd's mom." Todd looked at his grandfather and saw his face soften and his eyes glistened with pride.

White curls bobbed up and down as Haley leaned over to look through the tendrils of soft yellow clouds. She loved watching Todd's mother.

"She isn't so sad today," she said. "She's crying in that sweatshirt, but she doesn't feel so sad."

They watched as Alice started digging, planting bulbs, and gently tamping the ground.

When she turned her face upward, Todd thought she looked right at him. She closed her eyes, and her lips transformed into a smile as white flakes began to tap gently on her face and all around her on the ground.

"I love your mommy. I wish she were my mommy." Haley was leaning over a wall of clouds, longingly looking towards the earth, as snowflakes began to fall.

Behind him, Todd could hear the cacophony of laughter as the little ones gobbled their ice cream.

"Hey, save some for me!" Grandpa Carl yelled, winking at them both.

"Let's go get some ice cream before it's all gone." Todd reached out his hand towards Haley.

"Okey-dokey," Haley said, taking his hand and jumping among the clouds. Todd noticed she was looking over her shoulder at his mother below. A warmth spread through him as his mother tried to catch a snowflake on her tongue. They used to do that together when he was younger. She looked happy. She looked at peace.

"No, wait!" Haley stopped him. "I got an idea! I know how to get real ice cream. I bet your mommy would buy me all the ice cream in the world!"

Just like that, in a mist of snowflakes and a puff of pale yellow, Haley was gone.

CHAPTER 9

HELLO

Standing for a moment in the crisp December morning, Alice shut her eyes and welcomed the warmth of the sun on her face. But a shadow crossed over as the wind whipped her hair and when she opened her eyes, she saw the darkening clouds slowly encompass the sun. She reached for her gardening gloves, grabbed the trowel and shovel and placed them in the box of bulbs.

She grabbed Todd's navy Nike sweatshirt which was always hanging on a hook by the entrance door. She slipped it over her head, and the scent of her son teased her memory. She held the collar to her nose, breathing deeply.

She slowly sat on the cement floor to allow the memories to sweep through her. She had read somewhere, "Grief is like an ocean, it ebbs and it flows." Breathing deeply, she allowed the flow to crash over her.

She chose the spot where the bench nestled right under the leaves of the Dwarf Japanese maple tree. This was a place where Todd would sit in the evenings, and sometimes she would join him and they would talk and sometimes they would just sit quietly.

Laying the boxes of bulbs on the mulch under the bench, she stooped to sort them. She was not one to organize groups of colors like they showed in gardening books, although those arrangements were beautiful. She loved the freedom of the wildflowers in fields. Nature at its best.

As she kneeled, she touched a leaf of the fiery maple tree. Then she began to dig holes, enjoying the touch and smell of the rich, dark soil. Something cold touched her forehead. She looked up as little flecks of snow started falling around her. Shutting her eyes, she let the small, cold flakes gently touch her cheeks. She stuck out her tongue to catch a snowflake.

"What are you doing?" a soft voice asked.

Startled, Alice turned to see a little girl with almost white curls and bright blue eyes standing right next to her. Her cherub face was flushed and she wore a questioning smile.

Alice looked at her and then looked around the yard, next door, and up the driveway to see if anyone else was there. Not a person or a car in sight.

Alice leaned back on her heels and noticed that the little girl was totally unprepared for this weather. She was wearing a yellow dress with ruffles along the bottom and a bow at the waist. She had no socks, but wore little white feathery slippers on her feet.

"Are you by yourself? Where are your parents?"

"I don't have any parents."

Alice again glanced around at the empty neighborhood.

"Well, actually, I do have a mommy and daddy, but they don't want me anymore. So, I want you to be my mommy!" The little girl's excitement was authentic and Alice wasn't sure what to do. She stood, brushed her hands, and stooped to talk to the little girl.

"What's your name?"

"Haley Margaret Jensen," she replied, proudly, chin up with her hands on her hips.

"Well, Miss Haley Margaret Jensen," Alice said, reaching for her hand. "My name is Alice, and we have to find where you belong." She started to walk towards the house next door that shared the driveway, but Haley held back.

"I belong here," she said, again. "I want *you* to be my mommy."

Alice smiled as they reached the front door and knocked. The little girl squeezed her hand.

"This is not my home," Haley whispered in a sing song voice.

Alice nodded and turned to the opened door.

Her neighbor of 25 years smiled at both of them.

"Hi, Alice," she said, welcoming. "Is this one of your nieces?"

"I'm Haley," the little girl said, hands behind her back, rocking from toe to heel.

"Actually, Dana. I was hoping she was with you. You don't recognize her?"

"No," Dana said. "I've never seen her. You don't know her?"

"She just came up to me a few minutes ago. I don't know where she came from." Alice felt another squeeze of her hand.

"This is my mommy," Haley told Dana, leaning into Alice's legs. Alice looked at Dana, and said, "Well, I think we'll take a walk to see if anyone is looking for her."

Dana called," Let me get my sweater. I'll help you look."

The three of them started up the long driveway towards the main street. Alice saw Ben's SUV turn onto the driveway. He stopped and rolled down his window.

"Hey, ladies," he said, looking at Alice. "Who's your little friend?"

Alice cringed, trying to contain a surge of irritation at the smell of alcohol on his breath. "She just came up to me while I was planting bulbs. We're taking a walk to see if anyone is looking for her."

Ben pulled the truck to the side of the driveway, putting it in park. Stepping down from the car, he asked, "How can I help?"

Alice's anger melted as she saw the forlorn look on her husband's face. Her frustration would have to wait. Hate the disease; love the alcoholic.

"I was going to walk across the street to see if I can find her parents." Dana indicated she would go left, and Ben said would go right.

Ben leaned down to speak to Haley.

"And who are you, young lady" he asked. Haley scrunched up her face and turned her head away, squeezing Alice's hand.

"I'm Haley, and you are supposed to be my daddy, but I don't want you if you have al-co-hol breath."

Stunned, Ben looked up at Alice, who just shrugged, holding back a sad smile.

"Well, I'm going to help you find your parents, all right?" He stood and for one of the few times in his life, he blushed.

"All right. But you won't find them," Haley sang.

They walked through their neighborhood, knocking on doors for almost an hour. Alice went down to the neighbors who were having the party, but no one recognized Haley. They all met back at the top of the street and decided to call the authorities.

They started walking back down the long driveway that led back to their homes. Alice thanked Dana for her help, assuring her they would let her know what happens. Ben walked past his SUV, glancing at Alice, nodding. Haley bounced ahead of them, skipping to the front door of Alice's house, waving goodbye.

Ben pulled out his cell phone and started to dial.

"Who should I call?"

Alice shrugged and replied, "What about the detective that came here when Todd died?? I've got his number. He said to give him a call if we need anything. This is kind of an emergency, right?"

"What will you tell him?"

Alice stopped before opening the front door. For a moment, everything seemed normal. The old normal. When they could talk to each other about simple things that were important or did not matter.

She shrugged. "I guess that a little girl just came up to me and we can't find her parents?"

As she stepped inside the house, Haley looked around in awe as she moved into the kitchen.

"It's exactly how I knew it would be..." she said, delighted. She clapped her hands together and danced into the kitchen. She stopped to look at the display of photos on the front of the refrigerator. Glancing over all the photos, she stopped at one and pointed her finger at a photo.

"That's him! That's my friend!"

She pointed to the picture of Todd in his college baseball jersey. Alice glanced at Ben with a bewildered look. Ben shrugged his shoulders.

"I'll call that detective. I think his name is Matthews," she said, looking though the address book she kept by the phone. She found the business card taped to the inside cover and dialed.

Haley looked up at Ben and said, "I'm hungry."

"Well then, let's get you something to eat," Ben said, heading to the pantry. Looking over his shoulder at Alice, he raised his eyebrows. He reached into a cupboard and grabbed a bag of Trail Mix.

Alice spoke with the detective, explaining the situation. There was a long pause while Alice answered in short words. Yes, the little girl looked healthy but underdressed. Yes, she said her parents didn't want her. She was told there were currently no missing children in the local database, and nothing had come through nationwide. Matthews would contact social services and he would meet them at her house.

Alice started explaining to Ben what the detective had said as she walked through the kitchen towards the family room. Ben was sitting on the couch and not in his usual recliner. She glanced at his recliner and saw the tops of white curls bouncing above the seat.

Haley turned to look at Alice, saying, "This is one of my favorite shows. Daddy found it for me."

They were watching a cartoon with a little pink pig speaking with a perfect British accent. She was jumping in mud puddles with her little brother, who had a green dinosaur. Alice had never seen the show before. She glanced at Ben, who was as confused, and entranced, as she was.

"I think it's called Pippa or something." Ben's leg was crossed and she noticed that he had a glass of water on the end table.

"It's *Peppa Pig!* Her daddy jumps in muddy puddles!'"

Haley was eating from a baggie filled with Trail Mix. She reached for the little cup of water next to her. She was entirely at ease, completely at home. Alice sat next to Ben.

"Well, this is nice," she commented.

"Will you come sit with me?" Haley asked.

"I don't think that seat will hold both of us very well," Alice replied.

Normally, it wouldn't bother her at all to sit with a niece or nephew or some little person she knew. She didn't think it would be a good idea for now. Haley seemed fine--she wasn't crying, and exhibited no signs of stress or worry. She acted like she belonged here.

Then there was her comment when she saw the picture of Todd on the refrigerator. How did this little girl know her son? Alice didn't know what to think. As Haley watched the television, she watched Haley, and her thoughts wandered.

When the doorbell rang, both Alice and Ben stood up, and Alice moved instinctively beside Haley. Ben went to open the door. He escorted a familiar detective and two people from the county social services into the family room.

It was Elliot Matthews, one of the detectives who had responded the morning Todd died.

"Detective," she nodded.

"Actually, it's Lieutenant Matthews now," he said with a grin and shook her hand. He introduced the two women with him as representatives from social services. They were here to place Haley in a foster home until they could locate her parents.

"So, who do we have here?" Matthews stooped beside Haley. She looked at him, and then at the other people in the room.

"So, who are you?" she echoed.

"My name is Elliot. I've come to help you find your way back home."

Haley shook her white curls shook back and forth, and folded her arms across her chest.

"Oh, no. This is my home now."

Alice shrugged her shoulders when he looked up at her.

"Where are your parents?"

Haley's shoulders sagged as she pressed closer to Alice.

"They don't want me."

"Who doesn't want you, your parents?"

She nodded, and then said something that made everyone in the room uncomfortable.

" Yes. They were mean to me and I...." she paused a moment, wondering if Heaven was a big secret down here. "They gave me away." She rocked back and forth on her feet. "They didn't want me."

"Where do you live?"

"I don't know. I'm only six years old!" She spread her fingers as she tilted her head. "I think maybe Ohio?"

"Well, Miss 6 years old," Matthews continued. "How did you get here?"

She shrugged her shoulders in response.

Lieutenant Matthews stood for a moment and moved to Alice and Ben. Alice was explaining to the social workers how Haley had just shown up earlier, while Alice was planting bulbs. The little girl was by herself.

"We'll have to take her with us," said Matthews, "until we figure this all out. But I need to ask her a question. No offense." They both nodded and Matthews stooped down in front of Haley one more time.

"Haley, did these people take you from your home and bring you here?"

Alice reached for Ben's hand, sensing where this was going.

"Oh, no...!" Haley said, looking at Alice. "I just came up to her and told her I wanted her to be my mommy."

Alice smiled wanly at Haley and nodded in agreement. "I was planting bulbs."

"Well, then," a female social worker said. "Haley, you need to come with us so we can find where you belong."

Tears welled in Haley's eyes as she jumped from the chair and buried her face in Alice's legs. Alice reached down to touch her shoulder.

"No! I don't want to go with you! I want to stay here! I want her to be my mommy!"

Alice glanced at Ben.

"Can we just keep her here until you find out who she is and where she belongs?" Alice asked.

"No, ma'am," Matthews replied. The lady reached out to Haley and gently pried her arms away, softly reassuring her that things will be fine.

Alice walked behind them as the lady carried Haley to the foyer. Both the social workers gave her their business cards.

Ben moved ahead and opened the front door. It was dusk by now, and there was a light blanket of snow on the ground. He stepped aside as the others walked outside.

"Oops!" the social worker said as she stumbled off the step. "I almost stepped on that frog."

Haley's eyes brightened. She jumped from the lady's arms and stood over the creature, staring down with eyes and mouth wide open.

"It's not a frog! It's a toad!" She bent down and carefully touched the back of the little brown toad. It did not jump.

It just sat still.

"He's beautiful," Haley whispered. Alice looked at the toad that still appeared every now and then, and then back at Haley. She had no idea what was happening.

One of the ladies from social services buckled Haley into a car seat. The little girl's lip trembled, but there were no tears.

Alice turned to Ben as they watched the cars pull out of the driveway. He was staring down at the little toad, still in the same spot.

"You think...?" His words drifted with his thought. Alice offered him a wondering smile.

"I have no idea," she said as she turned to go inside. "Nothing makes sense. Who is she and and how did she know Todd?"

"And the toad," Ben said. "There is something about that toad."

They walked together to the kitchen and looked at the photo on the refrigerator, neither saying a word.

"Well," Alice sighed. "I'm going upstairs to check my email and Facebook. What are you going to do?"

She hoped he wouldn't drink, although after what just happened, she wouldn't be surprised if he did.

"I'll be up in a little bit." He looked at her, solemnly.

"Sorry. I never made it to the meeting. I started thinking about Todd. No, I don't have anything here. I just went to Sonny's Bar."

He paused with a curious smile and said," You know what she told me when we were watching TV?"

Alice saw a look of wonder in his eyes.

"She said I shouldn't drink any more al-co-hol." He accentuated the words just like Haley had done. "She said I can be her daddy if I don't drink alcohol anymore."

He studied Alice with raised eyebrows.

He paused, then continued.

"Is this some trick to make me stop drinking? Did you hire that little girl to get under my skin?"

He faked a questioning squint.

Alice looked squarely at him. "Would that be so bad?"

"You know I'm trying."

"Actually, I don't know that. How can you say you're trying when you leave to go to a meeting and then go straight to a bar?" She sighed, heavily, not wanting to engage in *this* conversation tonight.

"Alice," he implored, and she stopped to look at him. "I will try again. Starting tonight. I'll start going to meetings for real and clean up and get back to work."

"Did you even see the person you were going to meet for a job?" She knew the answer before she asked. His sheepish expression only annoyed her. She was getting tired of that grin that he hoped would make her smile in return. After years of promises and starts and stops, and no real effort, she knew his commitment would be gone with the next emotion he could not handle.

Alice nodded and continued up the stairs. Ben turned to go into the family room.

She paused at the top of the stairs, listening for the rustling sounds of a paper bag that told her he was sneaking a drink. The alcoholic in her understood him. As easy as it was to stop drinking (she herself, could stop at any time) the problem was that she couldn't *stay* stopped. After a few days, she would convince herself that one drink would be okay. But that one drink would never end. The insane cycle would start all over again until she tried to stop once more.

Yet the mother inside her who chose recovery almost five years ago was frustrated at his efforts. As hard as it was to finally commit to sobriety, it was becoming more and more difficult to understand why he didn't *want* to stay sober. It was baffling even to her why, after eight or nine months of sobriety, he convinced himself he could safely drink again. That was the insanity she understood; but she had a difficult time understanding why *he* didn't get it.

She certainly knew how hard it must be for him since Todd died. She knew it was only through the tools she learned in recovery and her efforts to honor both sons that she had stayed sober since his death. It was not easy and she was not special. But she knew that there was nothing now that a drink would make better. She simply had to go through each day with her eyes and heart wide open and a faith in a higher power that would help her through.

Shaking her head, Alice sat on the bed and opened up her little blue computer. She thought about Haley. Where did she come from? How did she recognize Todd's picture? How did she know about the toad? Why did she insist she was her mommy?

What in the world was happening?

⚊⟨⊹⟩⚊

Alice opened her eyes, startled at a sound she heard coming from downstairs. The room was dark, and so was the sky that peeked through the blinds. She glanced at the neon light of the clock. 12:30 AM.

She held her breath and listened again for the sound that woke her from sleep. She recognized the British voices of that children's show Haley had been watching coming from the family room below.

Good grief. He's drinking and watching Peppa Pig!

She turned to bury her head in her pillow, and was startled at the deep snort that came from next to her.

She glanced over to see Ben turning on his side, mouth moving as he slept. She shook his arm, and he woke up, turning groggily to her.

"Did you leave the TV on downstairs? I hear Peppa Pig."

She watched Ben as he listened to the television, and they heard the quiet, familiar giggles coming from the family room below.

"I think we have company," he said, curiously. "What's going on?"

Moving to the door, Alice looked back and said, "I have no idea."

Haley was sitting in her now 'favorite' recliner, and she turned to them as they entered the room.

"Hi, mommy!" she exclaimed, all smiles. Alice knelt beside her, a firm expression on her face.

"Haley, how did you get back here?" she asked.

"I don't know how it happens. I just think it, and I'm here!"

The house phone rang, breaking the silence in the room. Ben answered and spoke in short phrases.

"Yes, Haley is here." *Pause.* "No, we don't know how she got here." He glanced over at Alice. "No, we were asleep and we've been home all evening." *Pause.* "We just woke up ourselves. She's down here watching TV." He raised his eyebrows as he looked at Alice. "Yes, we locked the doors." Another long pause.

Haley moved over so Alice could sit next to her in the recliner. She rested her head against Alice and within moments, she was asleep.

"Listen, can we just keep her here until the morning? Believe me, we have no idea what's going on, but she's just a little girl and she's falling asleep in my wife's arms. *Pause.* Yes, sir. We will be here in the morning. Thank you for understanding. It's not like we are strangers to the county or to you. You know who we are."

Alice snuggled into the blanket Ben offered, tucking it around Haley. She nodded as Ben asked if she wanted a bottled water. He set the water next to her and kissed her softly on the forehead. He stroked the top of the little girl's hair.

Alice swallowed hard as she recognized something in his eyes that she hadn't seen in a very long time. Even before Todd had died.

She saw the man she married so many years ago.

"Goodnight," she said, as he moved away.

"Oh, I'm not going anywhere," he said, settling down on the couch, covering up with a blanket. "The way she pops in and out, I'm going to make sure that if you leave, I go with you both."

Alice rested her head against the back of the chair and looked down at Haley. Holding this little girl, memories of hugging another little boy, so many years ago, swept over her. Blinking back tears, she laid her head on the top of Haley's curls; the soft scent and her quiet breathing brought her a sense of peace.

Alice sighed. She had no idea what was happening. Nothing added up, and there had to be some explanation. But for this moment, she wasn't going to think about anything at all. She closed her eyes and fell asleep, nestling into the chair, holding Haley safe in her arms.

⊨⊩

The chirp of the doorbell woke her and when she reached to hug Haley, she realized she was holding her own arms instead. Her heart began to race. Where had the little girl gone?

She glanced around the room and heard Ben in the front foyer, opening the door.

"Ben, is Haley with you?"

She stood, the blanket falling around her ankles. She looked at Ben as he entered the kitchen. Lieutenant Matthews was beside him, holding a sheet of paper.

"We have a court order to take Haley to the hospital for a complete check-up to make sure she's all right," he said.

"She fell asleep on my lap," Alice said, looking at Ben, trying to stop the fear creeping into her thoughts. "I didn't feel her get up at all." Her voice trailed as her gaze volleyed between Matthews and the two people with him.

"Mrs. Thomas," Matthews said. "I can't figure out how you got her here again, but this is getting out of hand."

"You think I don't know that?"

For the first time, Alice's voice echoed her fear. She moved past the group of people in her living room and started up the stairs. "I don't know where she is."

As Ben and Matthews went into the kitchen to look for Haley, Alice shot an anxious glance at the two social workers texting on their phones.

"Can you please help us look for her?"

They apologized, put away their phones, and started looking awkwardly around the kitchen. A movement from outside the house caught her eye, and Alice opened the front door. On the left side of the step was the little toad. Sitting right next to it was Haley. "Hi, mommy! I'm playing with Todd's toad. Well, he's not really playing. He's just sitting there like toads do. I'm talking to him and he's listening to me." Her voice was sweet--she was not at all aware of the commotion she just caused.

Alice called out to Ben, "She's here!" and moved to sit beside the little girl.

She cast Matthews a serious glance, who in turn glanced at both social workers.

"You didn't see her when you just came up to the door?" She recognized their expressions--she felt just as confused as they looked. *What is going on?*

Lieutenant Matthews stooped down to speak to Haley.

"Haley, are you OK?"

"Yes, but I'm hungry. Can I have breakfast?"

Alice looked into the child's bright blue eyes.

"Haley. Remember these people from yesterday? Mrs. Lacey was very worried when she found out you were gone. You need to go with them. I have some snacks you can take with you, but you can't stay here."

"Well, I told her I was going back to mommy," Haley replied, scrunching her nose and shaking her head. "She knew I was coming back here."

"But how did you get here?" Matthews asked.

"I don't know. I just wish it and then I'm here!"

"Mrs. Thomas," he said. "I don't know how you got her here, and I'm not going to do anything about it right now. Just let these people take her where she needs to go and don't have any more contact with Haley until we find out who she is, and where her parents are."

He reached for Haley's hand, and Alice encouraged her to go with him. She watched as Haley went to the car, saw the desperate eyes looking back at her as she was strapped into the car seat. Sadness enveloped her.

"I want to stay with you," Alice heard the quiet voice say as they had walked away.

The detective came back up the driveway and offered Alice another card.

"Just in case you need help dealing with the loss of your son," Matthews said, gently. Alice glanced down at the card. 'Letting Go and Moving Forward' read the words on the card. Underneath was information about grief counseling.

Alice watched as he moved down the sidewalk towards his car.

"She's not here!" one of the social workers declared as she looked in the back seat.

Matthews held his hands out to his side.

"What do you mean she's not here?" Matthews checked the mechanisms of the empty car seat. The buckles were still tight, but there was no Haley.

Alice caught her breath as Matthews looked towards her, frowning.

"Okay, okay. I don't know what the hell is going on, but this has got to stop," he said, exasperated.

"I've been trying to tell you," Alice said, earnestly. "I have no idea what's going on. And..." she handed the business card back to the detective. "It certainly isn't in my head. She just showed up. She just appears. I have no idea how or why."

As she turned to walk back inside, her maternal instinct kicked in.

"Haley," she called out. "I want you to come here to me right now." She had no idea why she said it or if it would even work. She heard a little sigh from upstairs, a giggle and a whisper, "Oh, all right."

Haley appeared at the top of the stairs and slowly started down, leaning against the wall, watching Alice carefully.

"Don't be mad at me, please. I'm just playing. I just want to stay with you. Todd said you were a good mommy." The moment she said it, Haley realized what she had done. Heaven was supposed to be a secret, she remembered. Her mouth opened in surprise.

Alice raised her eyebrows at the mention of her son's name. A smile tickled at the corner of her lips.

"Todd...." her voice trailed softly.

"I just want to stay here. I want you to be my mommy."

Alice felt the soft curls as Haley grabbed her and laid her head against her legs.

With a deep, exasperated sigh, Alice stood face to face with Haley, eye level with the little girl standing on the third step.

"Haley, please tell me what's going on. Where did you come from? How did you get here?"

Alice stopped talking, looking at the little girl. Haley's eyes were wide and her mouth gaped open as she peered through the side windows of the doorway.

"My friends!" she cried. Alice felt the little girl's hands on her cheeks as she implored," All my friends are here!"

With wide eyes and open mouth, Alice stared at the incredible scene that was happening in her front yard.

CHAPTER 10

UH-OH

"Houston, we have a problem."

Todd turned to see the older angel watching below, touching the feather pen to his lips. He arched an eyebrow at Todd.

"Notice anyone missing?"

Todd looked through the clouds and saw his mother on her knees, planting bulbs. A little girl with white curls and a yellow dress stood beside her. She was animated as she talked, and he saw his mom listening intently. He recognized Haley instantly.

He looked around him and then back at The Scribe, confusion furrowing his brow.

"How'd she do that?" he asked, hoping it was possible he could do it as well. He longed for a visit back on earth.

"Now, don't go getting any ideas, young man. She was not supposed to do that."

The Scribe sighed, a combination of humor and distress playing across his ancient face.

Todd watched as Alice stood and took Haley's hand. They went to his neighbor's front door and he watched Dana join them. They walked up the driveway. All along, Haley was skipping and laughing and talking. His father joined them. He assumed they were looking for Haley's' parents. Everything that followed played out like a movie, only this time, it didn't appear on the sky screen above. It was in the real world below.

Haley skipped beside his parents as they went into his house. His melancholy turned into sweet contentment when he saw his mother smile.

"Oh, yeah, right. You think that's funny?" The Scribe nudged Todd gently. Even he smiled as Haley settled into the recliner, speaking to Ben.

"She's giving him what for," The Scribe leaned into him. "About his drinking."

Todd snorted and continued to watch below. He didn't notice that more and more angels were gathering along the edge of the clouds, peeking through the swirls of mist at the scene below. Small chatter filled the air as each began to realize that their little friend, Haley, was on earth. In human form.

"What is she doing?" they asked. "How did she do that? Why does she get to go back? I wanna go, too!"

Many angels had gathered around Todd and The Scribe. Their small wings fluttered softly as they watched the detective and social workers come to the house and take Haley with them.

The buzz up in Heaven settled into a quiet sadness. The little ones slowly flitted through the clouds back to the Ice Cream Machine. Grandpa Carl turned the crank, and dainty cotton candy balls puffed out of a tuba shaped opening. The atmosphere became quiet as the angels tried to catch the cotton candy floating above them.

Behind them, a group of elders tossed baseballs back and forth to each other. Suddenly, softballs, rubber balls, balloons, and bubbles started popping all around, mingling with the fluffy cotton candy. Todd nodded at the welcome distraction from what they were seeing below.

In an instant, the little ones started dancing around gleefully, chasing balls, bursting bubbles, and catching cotton candy in their mouths. After what seemed like hours, they finally settled down on their billowy beds and gently floated as darkness fell upon them.

Having no sense of time in Heaven, Todd realized he must have slept, because he was awake now and so were many of the elders. The little ones were still swaying gently with their dreams.

Todd's attention was almost always on Earth. He watched as several cars pulled up in front of his house. It was early morning and as the people walked into his home, he saw Haley holding onto his mother. He heard the rustling of wings behind him as little ones began to stir from their cloud beds. One by one, rubbing sleepy eyes, they joined him at the edge of the cloud wall, watching as Haley was once again buckled in the car seat. They all observed the detective's bewildered face as he turned away, then turned back to the car and realized Haley was no longer inside.

Todd felt the swishing of the air as it rustled all around him. The excitement was electric. From the eager whisperings and giggles, and the goosebumps tickling down his arms, Todd realized something was about to happen.

One by one, each of the angels disappeared in a puff of mist and anxious laughter.

"Oh, no you don't, little guys," The Scribe said, dropping his feather pen. "You can't. You just can't. You can't go down there."

Todd watched as the children trickled onto earth like snowflakes, drifting here and there until they landed in his front yard. He heard a chuckle come from deep within himself as they ran and skipped and danced and slid upon the snow-covered ground. He was laughing, himself. Finally.

But he heard the worry in The Scribe's tone.

"Uh- oh," The Scribe said, exasperated. He sat on a cloud and looked up at Todd. "Now we've done it." He sighed long and loud. "Well, actually, I've done it." He raised his eyes upward, speaking to someone unseen. "Yeah, yeah. I know. AGAIN!"

Todd's parents stood in the doorway with their mouths opened. When Haley brushed past them to join her friends, Todd saw a look on his mother's face that he hadn't seen since the night before he died. He watched her drop to her knees, eyes wide, and his heart swelled when he saw her beautiful smile. His father stood over her, hands against the sides of the door, incredulous.

"It was your stories," Todd heard The Scribe say. "I should have remembered. It happened only one other time, a long time ago."

Todd remained entranced by the scene below. He glanced at The Scribe and the forlorn look on his face gave him goosebumps.

"What?" Todd asked, innocently.

"They loved your stories. We have a job to do. We need to get those angels back here, before this is all over the news. Can you imagine what will happen if the press gets hold of this? "He rolled his eyes, and chuckled. "They'll have a field day with this. These children are angels. They are not supposed to be down there. If their parents catch wind...." He glanced over at Todd with consternation.

"What?" Todd leaned back, catching that look.

"They'll think their children are still alive, even though *they know what happened to them.*"

The Scribe let out a long sigh.

"You know what we have to do, don't you?"

"Go get them."

Todd swallowed with anticipation of going to earth and seeing his family again. He imagined the happiness he would feel hugging his family and friends again and seeing their great surprise.

Hey, he's back! He never died! It was all just a bad dream! We love you, Todd! We missed you! Welcome home!

His eagerness was silenced by The Scribe's next words.

"We can't go in human form. Well, I can, but not you."

"Why not?"

The Scribe looked at him steadily.

"You think we'll have problems with their parents recognizing them? What if *your* parents see you? It would upset the universe and the balance and all that. That goes for your parents even more so. How would they feel if you suddenly appeared to them, and then, in a few days, just went away again? "

"I could pop in and out...maybe?"

The Scribe rolled his eyes and said, "It's just not that easy."

"I would have a chance to say goodbye. I could tell them it was my time and that I'm okay with everything."

Todd swallowed to quell the sorrow that overcame him.

"It just can't be done. That's all." Todd looked at the elbow the Scribe offered to him, and linked his arm through it. "Sometimes this job just sucks," The Scribe offered, patting Todd's arm.

"Oh, and another thing," he stopped. "You can't get closer than a few feet from anyone, even in what we call 'spirit form.' That's the only time they might see you. If the light is just right, and, of course, if they *want* to see you, they will. Some aren't ready to believe anything just yet. Seeing you might just make a man drink." He winked at Todd. "Grief is handled in different ways as you can see. So, stay back. It's okay."

Todd nodded as The Scribe raised his eyebrows, waiting for a response.

"Okay!" Todd conceded.

"No closer than six feet." The Scribe said, and closed his eyes. "One more thing."

Todd stared at The Scribe, holding back his exasperation.

"Stay near me, so that no matter what happens, you will be safe."

Todd nodded, but then asked, "Safe from what?"

The Scribe gave a wry smile and straightened his shoulders. "Let's go!"

Todd's eagerness to join his family exceeded any worry about his own safety. He straightened his shoulders, took a deep breath, and shut his eyes as he was told. His heart pumped faster as he fell slowly through the sky. The task at hand was all that mattered now. One single thought passed through his head.

He was going home.

CHAPTER 11

LITTLE VISITORS

Haley brushed past Alice and stood in the middle of the doorway, watching with excitement at the scene in the front yard. Snow was falling in huge flakes as one, two, three children suddenly appeared, floating gently to the white-laced lawn. Alice could not believe what she was seeing.

It was snowing children.

"Stephen!" Haley said, excitedly, clapping her hands. "It's my friend, Stephen! Can he stay here too? He didn't have a good mommy or daddy, either."

A little boy, around the same age as Haley, dropped a snowball when he heard his name. He was dressed as simply as Haley—tank top, shorts and bare feet. He looked at Haley shyly and lifted a soft hand in hello.

A commotion of happy voices suddenly filled the air in front of her house. Alice watched as Haley ran out onto the front yard, hugging and skipping, squealing gleefully as more children appeared on the snow-covered lawn.

"Oh, my God." Alice caught her breath. Haley ran up to her, eyes sparkling, her cherub lips spread in a gleeful grin as she grabbed Alice's hands, jumping up and down.

"They're here! All my friends are here! Can we keep them? Can they stay?"

Alice slowly slumped onto the front steps, watching as Haley took the little boy's hand and ran to join the growing number of children appearing on the front lawn. Some were throwing snowballs, sliding on bare feet down the slippery hill. Others were just sitting in the snow, touching it softly, wonder in their eyes.

"We can't keep them, you know." Ben leaned down to whisper in her ear. She looked up at him, recognized the twinkle in his eyes. She nodded, not able to say anything.

Alice glanced up at Lt. Matthews who had stepped outside. Behind him, the two social workers stood in the doorway, their wide eyes and opened mouths expressing the same wonder. No one said a word. There was nothing that could be said.

Matthews pulled out his cell phone to call for back up. Alice smiled as she listened as he tried to explain what was happening. He asked for officers and social workers, and noted that maybe the FBI should come along, as well. Alice realized by the urgent tone in his voice that this was a very complicated situation. He glanced at her with a wry smile. "'Might as well send in the Calvary," he said.

"Maybe you should call someone else," Ben said wryly and looked up towards the sky. Alice smiled at his words, hugging her knees to her chest, watching as more and more children landed on her front lawn.

"What should we do?" she asked herself out loud.

"Let's get them inside," Matthews said, looking at the two women behind him.

Alice felt a hand slip into hers and soft curls tickled along her arm. She looked down at the little girl with sparkling eyes and slowly began to understand. Somehow, all these children are here because of Haley.

"I'll get everyone to come inside," Haley reassured her, and Alice looked down at her, realizing she was again reading her thoughts.

"Call Adam." Ben nodded. She had no idea what was happening, but Adam would help ground her as he witnessed this incredible event for himself.

⚔

The pattering of little feet sounded like the fluttering of wings as children cheerfully ran around her home. Some looked at the photos on the refrigerator and on the walls. Others sat in front of the television set, while still more jumped on couches and bounced on chairs.

Not knowing quite what to do next, Alice said to the group behind her, "Maybe I'll make a fresh pot of coffee."

She busied herself with measuring the coffee, filling the tank. She felt a quick kiss on her cheek and turned to see a little boy sitting on the counter next to her. In a blink, she thought she saw wings, but in an instant, they were gone.

"You're a funny mommy," the little boy said. "Can you snort for me?"

Alice stood there, empty pot in hand. *Please, help me understand. Please tell me I'm not going crazy.* She quickly prepared the coffee, watching the little boy out of the corner of her eye.

She felt soft curls against her legs and heard Haley say, "No, Stephen. She's *my* mommy. Yours is on the way." Alice watched them both skip out of the room.

The beep of the coffeemaker and the smell of coffee pulled her back into reality.

"Coffee's ready," she said, trying to make her voice calm, as if everything that was happening at the moment was normal.

She leaned against the island counter next to Ben and watched as the children began to settle down in front of the TV that Haley had turned on.

Alice turned to the others, waiting for someone to speak.

One of the women who stood by said, "Maybe we should order a pizza?"

"I can do that," Ben said, too quickly. "That I can do."

"How many children are here?" asked Matthews.

"Does it really matter?" Alice replied as Ben grabbed his car keys and headed out the front door.

Haley ran to him and touched his leg. "Daddy, don't go. You don't have to go."

Alice noticed his face turning red as he looked down at the little girl.

"I'll be right back with more pizza than you could ever eat."

"Stay here," Alice uttered.

She saw tears well up in his eyes.

"Maybe you should order delivery," Ben said quietly, and Alice could tell by his expression and the tone of his voice that he wouldn't be back for a while. "I'm sorry, Alice. I'm not as strong as you. I don't know what the hell is happening."

She watched as Ben got into his snow-covered SUV and started backing up. He passed Adam's car coming down the driveway.

"Mama Dukes!" Adam called as he and Lindsay came into the house. "Where's dad going?"

Alice looked at Adam, frustrated.

"He's not bringing pizza, is he," a little voice whispered.

She looked down at Haley, and smiled weakly. Then turned to Adam.

"Thank God you're here," she said, motioning to the children who were all around the family room. "Would you order a few pizzas? Then I'll explain. Maybe. If I can." She smiled wryly at her son as he turned to his cellphone.

"Adam, where did all these children come from?" Lindsay asked in disbelief.

Alice, Matthews, the two ladies from social services and Lindsay were staring at the family room where almost two dozen children were sitting around everywhere, watching Peppa Pig.

"Let's watch that one again," Haley said, as she moved past them to get the remote.

"What are you doing, mom? Collecting children?" Adam was by her side. The twinkle in his eyes reassured Alice that this phenomenon was as entertaining as it was completely surreal.

"Did you order the pizza?"

"Yep."

"How many?"

"Hmmm. About ten large pizzas with extra cheese." He smiled, and looped an arm around his wife. Lindsay was staring at the children, mouth opened in pleasant surprise. Haley stood up from her favorite recliner and crossed the room to join Alice. She grinned widely as she raised her neck back to look up at Adam.

"You're a giant."

Adam laughed, "I guess I am to you!"

Alice lifted back her shoulders as Adam looked at her, and then around the room.

"Adam, this is Haley."

"Haley Margaret Jensen," Haley corrected politely. "You're Adam. You're my big brother now!" She leaned into him, holding him around his legs, resting her head gently on his knees.

"I have a sister now?" Adam raised an eyebrow, eyes twinkling. "That was fast, mom."

The twinkle in his eye comforted her again. She felt a soft sparkle within herself that told her this was something special, out of the ordinary, magical, and she felt an overwhelming sense of calm.

Just then, Alice noticed two sets of headlights coming down the driveway, one behind the other. The pizza had arrived. So, did two other people.

Adam took the boxes of pizzas from the delivery man, and the room erupted with excited voices as he carried the boxes into the kitchen. Alice signed the credit card slip. The pizza driver passed two tall men dressed in black suits as they came up the sidewalk. She called to Lt. Matthews, and he joined her at the door.

One of the agents flashed his badge and introduced himself as an agent with the FBI.

"Lieutenant Matthews. You say you have some children who just showed up here today?"

Matthews began to explain the situation when behind her, Adam called his mother's name.

"Mom. I think you should come here."

Alice looked at Adam who stood in the kitchen, facing the family room.

"I think they're leaving."

Alice quickly went into the kitchen and saw each child, one by one, disappear. One moment they were sitting there, the next moment, nothing. No poof, no vapor, just gone.

Empty boxes of half eaten pizzas were the only proof that whatever had just happened was real.

Matthews came up beside her, the group of officials behind him.

"What the hell just happened?" Matthews breathed.

Alice shook her head, a slight smile playing across her lips.

"A miracle?" she answered.

Silence filled the foyer. No one knew what to say. Matthews spoke with the others and as they prepared to leave, he looked at Alice and Adam.

"We'll be back tomorrow." He shook his head and sighed.

Alice slumped against the door as she closed it behind them and looked at Adam.

A sudden panic spread through her and she called out for the little girl who first appeared-was it just yesterday?

"Haley!"

She instinctively ran up the stairs to her bedroom. The door was locked.

Alice knocked gently. "Haley," she whispered, praying the little girl was still there.

Adam reached for the lever over the door and unlocked it easily.

Alice exhaled deeply, blinking back the tears.

Lying flat on her stomach in the middle of the bed, arms outstretched and sound asleep, was Haley.

Alice stumbled against Adam, who kept her from falling. She felt tremendous relief that this little girl, with the soft white curls and angelic nature, was still here. She hadn't gone with the others.

"Want me to go look for him?" She knew who Adam was referring to.

"No. How sad is that, when you have to go looking around in bars for your dad?"

Alice lay carefully on the bed, gently placing her arm around the sleeping girl.

"You know where everything is," she said. "I'm just going to lay here with her."

"I think she plans on staying," Lindsay said.

Alice nodded and waved a hand at them.

"You both go home and get some rest. I'm going to let her sleep. Tomorrow, I'll take her to a store to get her some warmer clothes. She's been wearing that yellow dress since yesterday, but she never seems cold."

Adam nodded. "We will clean up first, just in case it doesn't clean up by itself." He grinned at her, gave her a hug and he and Lindsay went downstairs.

Alice laid next to her, fingers gently twirling the little girl's curls while she listened to the clean-up going on downstairs. She heard the beep of the security bell and then the starting of an engine. Alone for the first time since everything happened, she brushed back the white curls, listening to the soft breathing.

Alice rested her head on her arms, gazing into the growing darkness of the room, trying to figure out what had just happened.

She needed time to think about it before talking anymore. She wasn't fearful and something within told her that this was more than just amazing or impossible. This little girl knew Todd. She thought about Ben being out on this snowy night, but she felt too emotionally and physically drained right now to worry. She had no control over whether or not he drank; just as she had no control over what had just happened today. She was too tired to worry about anything now. Ben was a big boy, and he could take care of himself.

The home phone rang in the quiet. Answering it, she turned on the light switch and saw Caller ID. It was Adam.

"I think I know where one boy is." There was a mix of concern and amusement in his voice. "I think his name is Stephen. Evidently Haley told him we were his newer better parents and Mom.... he's buckled in a car seat. We don't have a car seat. He's sitting in the back seat. We just noticed him when he said, 'Let's go to your house'."

Alice sat up and dropped her legs over the edge of the bed.

"So...what are you going to do?"

"We're almost home. He can stay with us and we'll bring him over in the morning. You okay?"

"Yeah, actually I am. I don't know what's going on, but for some reason, I feel all right."

She hung up the phone and reached for the picture of Todd she kept on the nightstand. They had gone to the Redskins game together and they were both goofing for the camera. It was the last picture taken of them together. He had died a week later.

As she touched his wonderful smile, a sweet melancholy peace eased through her.

"Thanks, Todd. For whatever this is," she whispered.

She jumped in the shower, standing under the welcoming warmth with eyes closed, thinking about nothing at all. She put on her flannel pajamas and slipped under the covers. She took one of the blankets at the foot of the bed to cover Haley. She closed her eyes and went to sleep, not aware that for the first time in months, the television was silent.

The morning sun was glistening through the room when the house phone rang. Alice blinked in the bright light and reached to answer it. Haley turned and mumbled, snuggling closer as Alice moved.

"Mama D! Hey, I know where dad is. I just texted him. He's at Sonny's Bar. Did he stay out all night?"

"He texted me last night from the Inn. Said he was sorry." She paused. "Are you on your way?"

"We're stopping at McDonald's first. Someone is hungry."

Alice heard the clapping echo through the phone. "Want anything?"

"No. We're going to find something else for Haley to wear. We'll stop by to check on your dad before we get back. She paused. "I'm glad I still have that old car seat my friend gave me for when I volunteer." The moment she said the words, Alice realized something. "Isn't it funny that I still have that car seat in my car?" Her voice drifted as she thought about it.

"Yeah. Actually, it is."

Alice hung up the phone and turned to Haley, comforted by the serenity in his voice. Things were going to be all right.

"Haley opened her eyes and with a sleepy grin said, "Hi, Mommy. I didn't leave."

"I knew that you wouldn't."

"You're still here."

Alice smiled. "You knew that I would be."

Haley nodded sleepily, sitting up.

"Adam is coming with your friend, Stephen. I thought we could go buy something else you could wear and wash your pretty yellow dress before they get here. Would you like that?"

As she spoke, Alice realized how comfortable she was becoming about what was going on here. She noticed that when Haley sat up, not only did her curls fall into perfect place, but her yellow dress seemed as crisp and fresh as yesterday morning. The bow at her waist was tied perfectly.

"Can I get a mermaid dress? I always wanted a mermaid dress!"

She looked down at Haley and nodded. She wanted to say that Haley could have anything she wanted, but she held that in.

Alice found a sweater that had been put in the dryer by someone being helpful. It was no longer an adult size. She held it as Haley wriggled into it, flipping her white curls out of the collar. She then helped her put on a pair of her knee length socks. They went to the door and as Alice opened it, a burst of fresh cold air welcomed them as they stepped outside in the sunshine. The snow that had fallen yesterday was already glistening like frost in the warm sun.

Alice took Haley's hand. "Ready for an adventure?"

"Oh, I need my slippers!" Haley exclaimed and ran into the family room to get them. As she came back into the foyer, her hair bouncing along the collar of the forest green sweater that was still too big, her white feather slippers snug on her feet, Haley's smile was wide as she took Alice's hand.

Alice couldn't help but notice that not once did this little girl cry. Not once was there anything except the sparkling eyes of someone who was happy. As she buckled Haley into the car seat and opened the driver's door, she noticed something about herself.

She hadn't stopped smiling since the first time she met Haley.

CHAPTER 12
CUP OF JOE

Todd found himself in the middle of a dank, smelly alley. He looked down at Scribs, on his knees, struggling to stand.

"Can you help a fella up, please?"

Todd reached down, pulled the older angel to his feet, and looked around. There was something familiar about this place. He looked at Scribs, who was eyeing him carefully, trying to hide a smile.

"Geez, Todd. Don't you have anything else to wear besides that navy Shepherd sweatshirt?"

"I like it," Todd said simply. "Besides, my mom had just shown me how to sew the pockets back together. She wears this sweatshirt all the time now." He pushed his hands in the pocket, poking a finger through a hole he must have missed. "Besides, you're wearing a Cubs cap. We are in Nationals territory here. "

Todd ignored the grunt as Scribs straightened the blue baseball cap on his head. He took in the area where they had landed. The tall buildings cast shadows on brick walls. Empty boxes and bottles dotted the grimy ground.

"We come back to Earth in an alley?" Todd looked at Scribs.

Scribs shrugged as he kicked a can out of the way. "It's not like in the movies, where angels just pop up in hospital rooms or on streets. We're actually a little more discreet than that."

A heavy metal door opened, and a man came out dragging a large black trash bag. Todd nodded at the man, leaning towards The Scribe.

"Hey," Todd acknowledged.

"Hey," The Scribe repeated.

The man seemed startled, and blinked in the sliver of light as the morning sun peeked into the dark alley.

"Hey," he replied. "What are you doing out here? Don't be bumming in my garbage and making a mess."

Todd opened his mouth, but The Scribe spoke first.

"Hey, I'm just a regular guy like you. Just came back here for a smoke." His eyes twinkled. "You don't have a smoke on you, do you?"

"Yeah, I do." The man's face suddenly brightened as he took out a pack of cigarettes from his apron pocket. He offered one to Scribs. "Don't let them catch you out here smoking. I usually go up on the roof. It's a fire hazard or something and they will ticket you." He turned back to the door.

"Wait. Gotta light?"

Todd watched them exchange a few more words, and noticed that the man did not look at Todd at all. He waited anxiously as Scribs took a long drag on the lit cigarette, holding it in for several seconds before exhaling an exaggerated sigh.

"Hey, thanks, buddy," The Scribe said, and the man disappeared into the building.

Scribs inhaled one more time before tossing the cigarette on the ground and stomping it out with his foot.

"Sorry..." he said, sheepishly. "It's just been so long since I had a drag. The last time I had one of these we rolled them ourselves, ya know? What a rush that gave me."

Todd followed The Scribe as he walked down the alley, turned the corner, and walked up the sidewalk to the front door of Sonny's Sports Bar.

"Okay," The Scribe warned Todd "We gotta do this. I'm gonna try to convince someone to go home."

"People can see you, but not me, right?"

"Yep. If you start to feel a nagging compulsion to be human, just go into the bathroom."

"Why?" Todd asked, confused.

"Oh, brother," said The Scribe, rolling his eyes in feign exasperation. "For distance. You know? If *you know who* gets a look at you, well, it might give him a heart attack."

Scribs looked down the long counter at a man sitting near the end, head hanging over his glass, playing with his straw.

"Nah, he'll just think it's a delusion," The Scribe corrected himself, chuckling.

The Scribe took the stool next to the man, who was so far hunched over his drink that his head almost touched the rim of the glass. Todd felt the immense sorrow and frustration emitting from this man. He noticed the reflection of the man in the mirror behind the bar. He didn't recognize his father at all.

A flood of love and memories impelled him towards his father. This is what he was warned about. His father's sadness might transfer into Todd, and Todd would have to absorb it. In such a case, he could appear in human form. Actually, any emotion driven so deeply, Todd could absorb and appear. He had to keep his distance.

Todd took his place on the other stool, resting against the seat as he watched his dad order another dirty vodka martini. The ache in his heart grew stronger as the guilt amassed inside him. Even though Todd had come to accept that it was his time to go, he had never meant to cause this much pain. It wasn't his choice to leave. He felt only despair radiating from his dad. He felt the comforting pull of Heaven as his sadness mingled with his dad.

The Scribe leaned back to him and whispered, "This is not your fault! You dying didn't make him drink. He was already doing it. Remember that and lighten up!" Todd nodded, feeling his guilt lessen by The Scribe's kind words, this time void of sarcasm.

"Hey, man," The Scribe turned towards Ben. He grabbed him by the back of his head, pulling his face away from falling in the martini glass. "You don't want to go swimming in that drink, do you?"

"Actually, yeah. I wouldn't mind a bit," Ben mumbled.

Ben blinked several times, trying to focus on The Scribe.

"That's not healthy for you, you know." The Scribe answered. Todd watched his father's head lower back towards the rim of the glass. He nodded his head and continued staring down at his drink. "It's not like I want to."

"Say what?" The Scribe chuckled. "If you *didn't* want to drink you wouldn't be *here*."

"It makes me feel normal," Ben answered. "You have *no idea* what's going on in my world right now."

Todd stifled a smile as he watched The Scribe smirk.

"Oh, *you have no idea...*," he said as he looked up at the television. "What? Is the world coming to an end? No. Are there terrorists behind every bush? Maybe. Are aliens creeping out from under rocks and Zombies coming from cemeteries? Oh, wait! Yes! Any moment."

Todd felt something different as his dad looked up at The Scribe. His father's old humor surfaced as he let out the bellowing laughter Todd knew so well. It had been a while since he'd heard that sound, even before he died.

"I'm Ben," he said, he said, offering his hand.

"I'm not," The Scribe replied.

His dad grinned. "Hey, Chevy Chase. I like that."

Ben turned towards The Scribe.

"So, what's going on in your life?" Ben asked.

"My life is just fine—well, for the most part," The Scribe replied. "I was wondering why you were here on a Saturday afternoon, all by yourself and watching the *news!* What is so bad about your life that you are here and not somewhere else like maybe-*home*?"

Todd hoped his father would tell The Scribe exactly what haunted him every single day since he died. He understood his father more now than he ever had before. His dad held everything inside, trying to cope with reality by ignoring it completely. *Tell him,* he pleaded with his heart. *Tell him everything! Tell someone!*

"I don't even know your name." *Deflection, as usual.*

"Well….in a spiritual way, my name is The Scribe." Todd caught his glance and his careful smile. Scribs glanced up at the TV, smiling as he saw a man with silver hair and a kind smile appear on the screen. It was a morning talk show called, "A Cup of Joe."

"Joe…. you can call me Joe... Joe Scribs!" Todd shook his head, enjoying how easy it was for Scribs to relax in any situation. It must be nice to feel so comfortable as an angel.

Todd nodded at The Scribe, encouraging him to continue.

"So, Ben, what's so bad about your life that you are here on a beautiful afternoon getting drunk?"

"I lost my son a few weeks ago. He just went to bed and didn't wake up." His voice cracked as he explained it as if it was a normal thing to see.

Ben turned to Joe and rested his elbow on the bar, almost tipping his glass. For a moment, Todd thought his dad could see him. "A little girl showed up last night who knows Todd, and then a bunch of children just started appearing up at my house like—like it was snowing children!" He bobbed his head and pointed his finger at Joe, trying to make his point. "I try to not drink. I'm really trying. But I can't stop. I've tried, but I can't. Everything hurts so much." Ben turned back to sip at his drink.

"Well, you could if you really wanted to."

There was a long pause before Ben said, quietly, "I don't want to." He belched, and Todd smelled the vodka on his breath. "I just want to stop hurting. I just want to have fun again, and not hurt."

"Are you having fun now?" The Scribe asked. Todd felt his father's anger as he raised his head and looked at The Scribe.

"Who *are* you?"

Joe reached over and pushed the empty glass away from Ben.

Todd kept his eyes on his father.

"Right now, I'm your best friend," Joe whispered. "And in just a few minutes, you'll wish you were anywhere but here."

A tingle trickled down Todd's back as a feeling of comfort began to spread throughout his body. Studying his dad, Todd heard Joe whisper, "You have to get out of here, now!"

"Who, me?" Ben raised his head to look at Joe. Todd felt, with a touch of melancholy, his father looking right through him. But another emotion, much stronger than sadness, compelled him to look towards the large picture window that faced the parking lot.

A sense of peace overcame him even before he saw his mom. He watched her cross the street outside, holding the hand of a little girl.

Haley.

Feeling a sense of immense yearning, he moved away from the bar and found himself outside, by the front door.

He noticed Haley's eyes widen, and a grin crossed her face as she recognized him. But before she could say his name, he put a finger to his lips, smiled at her, and was gone.

CHAPTER 13

STRANGE THINGS

Alice opened the glass door for Haley and the little girl gig-gled as she went inside. As she allowed her eyes to adjust to the dim lights of the restaurant, she saw Ben at the bar. He was speaking with an older gentleman, leaning towards him in quiet conversation.

Alice felt a tug of emotion as Haley yelled, "Daddy!" and started to run towards the bar.

As both men turned to look at her, Haley stopped. Her arms dropped to her side, and she looked with wide eyes at the man sit-ting next to Ben. Alice noticed the hint of a smile as the older man turned to Haley.

"It's you!" Haley cried out, standing as still as a statue, arms glued to her side. She ran to the stranger, and Alice watched as the man leaned down to give the child an awkward hug. Alice fol-lowed, worried when she saw the man whisper something to Haley. She nodded and gently backed away. The excitement of a secret in her eyes, she moved shyly towards Ben.

As she stood between the two men, Alice noticed the twinkle in the old man's eyes as he looked at her. While she still felt a bit uncomfortable, there was something about his pleasant smile that eased her apprehension.

He shrugged himself off the stool, nodding towards Haley.

"Ah… she thought I was her grandfather," he offered by way of explanation. He extended his hand, and Alice shook it firmly, glancing at Ben.

"Ben, we've been waiting for you to come home." She measured her words carefully, glancing at the stranger who was still looking at her with a knowing grin. She turned to him with a quizzical look. "Do I know you?"

"I'm Joe," Joe greeted her with a smile. "And you are Alice."

He blinked. "Ben's been telling me all about you and your 'problem'."

She again noticed his twinkling eyes, and felt the familiarity he seemed to already have towards her. Alice glanced between Ben, Haley, and this man. It all seemed so oddly familiar and comfortable. The hair on her arms prickled.

"What 'problem' is that?" She watched her husband.

"About, you know, all those children showing up yesterday morning," Joe joked, glancing at Ben. "He actually said it was snowing children." He rolled his eyes, still watching Alice.

Alice saw the two men exchange a meaningful glance. Shaking her head, she glanced up at the TV screen, where regularly scheduled programming was being interrupted by a breaking news story. A red ribbon of information crossed the screen saying, "Missing Children Show Up at Local Resident's Home."

Alice swallowed and blinked several times as she instinctively moved behind Haley, wrapping her arms around the little girl's shoulders. Her eyes widened as she saw that the News Van was in front of *her house*, interviewing Matthews.

The reporter was asking Lieutenant Matthews if he had any updates about how all these children, presumed dead, had appeared here, in Woodridge Lake, at *this house. Alive.*

The detective looked into the camera as if speaking directly to Alice and Ben.

"This is an ongoing investigation, and I have no comment, except to say that there are no children here at this moment. They have been placed in protective services until their identities can be confirmed." Alice appreciated his easy lie.

The news reporter adjusted her earpiece and pushed the microphone back into his face.

"But that's not true. I'm now getting reports that some of these children are showing up everywhere. Some are at St. Margaret's Church, grocery stores, local schools....asking people to be their parents. One little girl is actually living in *this* house saying these people are her parents."

The ticking of a clock echoed in the silence of the restaurant. There was a phone ringing. Dozens of eyes were transfixed on the television.

The man turned to the reporter, looking directly at her.

"The FBI and the local authorities have cleared the Thomas family. They are not persons of interest in this investigation. Law enforcement are looking into this matter. They are as surprised as everyone else at what is happening."

"So, these children all just started showing up out of nowhere?" the reporter questioned in disbelief, trying to press the issue.

Lt. Matthews shrugged his shoulders and simply replied, "Yeah. That seems about right."

"I heard that you have consulted with church authorities. Do you think there is something unusual...that is, supernatural, about what is happening?"

The detective raised his eyebrows, and with a sarcastic grin, repeated, "Supernatural? No. Nothing like that." He paused, looking directly into the camera as if speaking to Alice and Ben.

"Maybe something far more...spiritual than that."

As more reporters began to crowd around Lieutenant Matthews, he moved towards his black SUV, avoiding the microphones jammed in his face, ignoring all questions. With a wave and no smile, he got into the car and shut the door.

The camera then panned back to the reporter, indicating a block in the corner of the screen, displaying photos of missing children from around the country. "It is suspected that many of these missing children might be here in Woodridge Lake."

Alice put her hand to her heart. The first photo was of Haley. The reporter explained how these children were presumed dead—most of them had funerals. The reporter faced the cameras and urged that if anyone recognized any of these children, or were related to them in any way, to please contact the FBI and local hotlines posted below.

"Mommy, that's me," Haley whispered.

Alice was suddenly aware of the thundering silence in the room as the bartender looked at all four of them.

"That's one of the little girls," the bartender said, simply.

"We need to get home, Ben," she said tersely. "Now."

"I'm in the doghouse again," Ben said wearily, pushing his glass away. Alice noticed that Joe was slowly moving the glass towards himself.

"You put yourself in that doghouse," she replied. She took Haley's hand and turned away.

Joe tipped his hand to Ben, acknowledging her words.

"The lady does have a point," he said.

Alice shot him a look over her shoulder as she walked towards the door, keeping Haley close to her. A woman and man stood in front of her, blocking her way.

"Isn't that the girl on TV?" the woman huffed. "What is she doing with you? Didn't the police take her from you?"

Alice ignored them as she pushed through the small group of people who had gathered at the front of the restaurant.

"Mommy, why are they so mad?" Haley looked at all the people, tears welling up in her eyes.

"Someone should call the police," a man exclaimed.

"Hey, hey....no need to do that."

Alice couldn't help but notice that Joe had downed that glass of vodka before joining them. He flashed the crowd a black wallet with a shiny gold badge.

"Calm down everyone. I *am* the police. I'm with the FBI and I'm escorting them home."

Slowly, Joe put himself between the three of them and the group of excited citizens that seemed to be growing larger by the minute. A constant click of cellphone cameras surrounded them as well.

"You all need to go back and finish what you were doing. I don't want to arrest anyone here for interfering with an investigation. "

Alice tried to smile as Joe called over to the bartender.

"Everyone's tab is on Ben!" He glanced at Ben, whose lop-sided grin showed he approved.

As they walked to her car, Alice looked over at him.

"You're not FBI," she stated clearly.

"Well," he said, with a wry smile. "I *used* to be a long time ago."

Alice buckled Haley into the car seat and turned her gaze towards Joe, who sat in the passenger seat. "That's a crime, you know," she said, as she slowly drove through the parking lot.

"Lady. I mean Alice," he said, sweetly. "I have friends in high places and …I think you should step on it."

Alice noticed him glancing over his shoulder. She saw several news vans starting to pull up in front of the restaurant as people gathered outside.

Alice pulled onto the main road and shot a glance at him.

"Do you want to drive?" She was beginning to like this man named Joe.

His eyes sparkled as he looked at her. "Nah, you're doing just fine. Just get out of here!"

Ben sat in the back seat, combing Haley's curls with his fingers.

"Let's go home," Ben said, laying his head against the seat.

Alice shot him a look in the rearview mirror as Joe turned in his seat.

"Not your call," they said in unison. She looked at Joe dismayed, and he smiled at her and nodded.

"Well, let's go."

"Where?" Alice asked quietly.

"Anywhere but your home," Joe said. "Matthews will agree with me."

Suddenly, her cell phone began to ring and she looked over at Joe before pressing the button for the speaker phone.

"Mrs. Thomas, have you seen the news?" It was the Lieutenant.

"Yes. We almost got mobbed when I went to find Ben."

"Don't come home, yet. It's ridiculous here. Do you have somewhere to go for a while?"

"Yes," she whispered, her mind scurrying through her options. Her stomach growled and she glanced at Haley in the back seat. "What's going to happen?"

"Right now, we are trying to find where all the children are. I suggest we all meet back at your house later this evening. We have no idea what's going on. Maybe some of these children can explain it to us. Especially Haley."

"I can!" came the squeal from the back seat. Alice noticed Joe Scribs had turned and put his finger to his lips and Haley quieted, knowingly.

Alice finished the conversation and turned off the street into a parking lot. Turning to Joe, she asked, "Please tell me what's going on!" She blinked several times as her voice gave way to her feelings.

"Don't cry, Alice." His voice was genuinely calming. "I promise as soon as we get all the children back to your house, everything will be explained." A chewing sound came from the back seat as Ben adjusted himself and began to snore.

"I know!" Joe said, looking back at Haley!" Let's get something to eat! I'm famished!"

Alice nodded as Haley looked down at Ben, sadly.

"Well then, who want's Mickey D's?"

"I do!" Two voices called out together—a little voice from the back seat, and one right beside her.

"I'd *love* some ice cream," Joe said. "I hear that in Heaven when they make ice cream, it *snows down here!*" He winked back at Haley, who started to smile brightly.

Alice looked in the rear-view mirror at her husband and her resentment toward him being drunk slowly dissipated into sorrow. He was staring out the window, head hanging, arm around the back of Haley's car seat.

Alice imagined that he too was remembering a little boy with his own curly blonde hair, who, long ago, sat in his own car seat.

"I don't like yellow hair," the little boy had said that day. "I want black hair." He'd realized that he didn't have the same hair color as his brother, mom, and dad.

Alice blinked back the tears as she remembered her response.

"Don't worry, Todd." She had said. "Your hair will get darker. I love your yellow hair. It's perfect. It's Todd."

People had asked her before why she didn't leave Ben, who was snoring from the back seat. That would have been so easy, she had thought. But there were months when he would stop drinking, when he tried everything-going to a therapist, meditating, going for a month to a recovery program or going to support groups. Her heart had been entwined with Ben's since they were twenty years old, and she understood him more now than ever. He was a good man with a hated illness, one she too had overcome. In the middle of an addiction, it is so hard to realize that one had a choice. She understood.

Ben slowly drifted back to sleep, his hand draped along the back of Haley's car seat.

Alice pulled into the drive-thru lane, turned to Joe, and asked if he wanted anything else besides ice cream.

"Hmm," he feigned decision. "You paying?"

Alice couldn't help but smile as he leaned in to look at the menu. Alice looked in the rearview mirror at Haley.

"Chicken nuggets okay with you?" She saw the yellow curls dance up and down. "And a vanilla milkshake, too?"

Alice turned as the person on the speaker asked for her order. She ordered the chicken nuggets for Haley, a bacon and egg biscuit for herself, and a chicken sandwich meal deal for Ben. She looked at Joe, who tried to act indifferent.

"Well... I'll take a Big Mac meal deal," he yelled to the speaker, leaning towards Alice. "Supersized with a coke." He looked in the back seat for a second. She glanced in the rearview mirror. She saw the reflection of the sunset, making her blink.

"Yeah, and a grilled barbecue chicken with cheese, hold the lettuce and pickles, add mayo...just the sandwich. And a vanilla milkshake, two strawberry pies...and..." Alice flashed him an exasperated look. "Uh, the chocolate chip cookies," he finished quickly.

Something in her stirred when Joe ordered the grilled barbecue chicken sandwich, holding the lettuce and pickles, adding mayo. It was Todd's favorite sandwich. She leaned back and looked at him, carefully. "Anything else?"

With that same sparkle in his eyes, he said, "Do you mind if I get a bottled water?"

"We're done," she said to the speaker, pulling forward.

They heard snoring from the back seat. Ben was now leaning against the window, a string of drool hanging from his opened mouth.

"Hey, don't blame me," Joe said, simply. "You married him."

Alice ignored the comment as she passed the bags and drinks over to Joe and pulled away.

"Can I have some fries now, please?"

"Yes, can I have some fries too...please?" Joe was looking at her imploringly. He reached into the bag and grabbed a mouthful of fries, stuffing them into his mouth before handing the box back to Haley. "Sorry," he apologized, mouth full of French fries. "I remember when they first came out with these fries," he mumbled as he chewed. "They were so greasy, you could lick your fingers forever."

They drove around town until Alice found a spot near a park down by the Occoquan River, not far from where she lived. It was quiet here and, even though it was mid-afternoon with the cold weather, they had the area to themselves.

Joe made enthusiastic comments about everything he saw. Alice realized that he was trying to keep her from noticing that Haley was talking to herself animatedly.

She leaned her head against the window, turning towards Joe. He ate every bite of his food, not stopping until he came to the very last cookie.

"Want the last one?" he asked her, his mouth full of cookies.

"Oh, no, please, you eat it." she said.

"Can Haley have it?" Joe asked. Alice nodded, and he reached back to offer it to Haley, then licked his fingers loudly. She had no idea whether he was teasing her good-naturedly, or just had absolutely no manners.

"Who *are* you?" She asked, firmly. She sat up to face Joe, while Ben snored and Haley began to snooze.

"A friend of Ben. *You know*...like Bill W."

"Did you meet him in the rooms?"

"Actually, I just met him at the bar. But I've seen him around."

There it was again, Alice noticed. That gentle, private, secret kind of smile. She shook her head and sighed. "Do you think he'll ever get it? This has been going on for years and at times, since Todd died, I don't know if I can take it. It's like living with Dr. Jekyll and Mr. Hyde sometimes."

She saw that twinkle in his eyes again.

"You did."

She grunted softly at his response. *Yeah, I did it because no one else could help me and I was losing everything and blacking out and thought I was going crazy and I didn't want to lose my mind.*

She saw him nod. "Yep," he replied. "That's because you are the responsible one."

Alice looked at him, realizing that he knew what she was thinking.

"Who *are you?*" She asked again.

"Someone who wants to see you all happy. Don't worry, Alice. He'll get it. Eventually. He really wants to stop drinking. He just doesn't think he can. He feels so weak, and he wants to control his drinking so much that he thinks the next time will be different. He only wants one or two drinks. But you know how that is."

She *did* know how it was. The saying goes, 'One drink is too many and a thousand is not enough.'

"He's disappointed in himself. He thinks he's a failure and that he failed you." Joe's voice grew quiet. "He thinks he's let your son down, too. He misses him a lot. Just doesn't know how to deal with it. He thinks he's being strong when he drinks."

"Yeah, liquid courage," she nodded. "I don't blame him because he's drinking," she said quietly. "He was drinking at the time. He thought we didn't know, but we did."

Alice turned the ignition and dropped her head. "I just don't understand why he doesn't see the damage that's being done. I miss my son. And I can't drink. It's not an option for me anymore. It's not fair. I just feel so alone. I'm just getting through because I *have* to."

She felt the softest brush of her hair. She reached up to touch the spot and looked at Joe. He was leaning against the window, arms crossed, looking out at the night.

"Nah..." Joe said, gently. "You're not alone. Ever."

She smiled weakly at him, glancing in the mirror at Haley sleeping in the back seat. She put the car in gear. They drove towards her home in silence.

The driveway was empty of all cars and vans as she pulled down to her house.

She turned to Joe and said, "I'm sorry. You never told me where to drop you off."

She saw the chocolate chip cookie crumb grin and felt so at ease with him, although he was still a stranger.

"Nah, that's okay," he said as he got out of the car, brushing crumbs from his pants.

"I'll help get *him* inside and then I'll go."

"Should I call you a cab?" She saw the leveled look in his eyes, and answered herself. "Guess not."

She reached in to unbuckle Haley as Joe opened the door on the other side. Ben startled awake as he stumbled out of the car.

"Oh, I'm sorry, did I wake you?" she heard the sarcastically kind voice quip.

Alice helped Haley out of the car and taking her hand, went ahead into the garage to open the door to the family room.

Joe carefully lead Ben up the short step into the house.

Alice took Haley upstairs, listening to the sounds below. She pulled out a pair of pajamas from the shopping bag and ripped off the tags.

She carefully changed Haley and tucked her into her bed. Alice brushed her curls as she leaned over and kissed her softly on the forehead. She stood watching her for a few moments, the ache in her heart reminding her of Todd, sleeping soundly, thumb in his mouth, soft yellow curls falling softly around his sweet face. She stood for a few moments, listening to Haley's easy breathing. Then she went downstairs.

Joe had set Ben down gently on the couch, and she smiled as he covered her husband with the same blanket that had covered Haley and herself two mornings ago.

"So, what are you going to do?" she asked as they walked through the garage.

"Well…I could stay here…" He trailed off, and she shot him a look. "But since you really don't know me, that would be a bad idea. I actually have some other place to be. I can come back and help with Ben, and um, Haley."

"I'd like that," she said. "It would be good for him to see you as a friend."

Alice watched with crossed arms as he walked away. He stopped, and turned towards her with a gentle smile.

"He's proud of you, you know."

Her heart skipped as she watched him, their shadows dancing in the late breeze.

"Who?"

"Your son. I just feel it. It's something I just…*feel*."

Joe tipped his hand in a salute and continued up the driveway.

Then, on impulse, he came back and gave her a quick kiss on the cheek. A light, gentle touch, nothing more.

"See you later, Alice!" He glanced towards the front door. "Don't forget to check on the toad."

He stood in front of the bench for a few moments, hands in his pockets. Then with a jaunt to his step, he made his way up towards the main street.

Alice stood, thinking about what he just said, then walked to the front porch to look for the toad. When she didn't see him, she turned back and called to Joe," How'd you know about the toad?" The driveway was empty, all the way to the main road up ahead. She glanced around the neighboring woods, but didn't see him. Just like that, he was gone.

She shrugged and walked back to the garage. The garage door creaked as it slowly closed the outside world.

The toad was just a small piece of a much bigger puzzle. She went upstairs, took a shower, and curled up onto her side of the bed. It didn't take long for Haley to snuggle up next to her. Alice gently stroked her hair.

She kissed the top of Haley's head, closed her eyes, said a prayer. She set the alarm on her cellphone for 45 minutes, in case she fell asleep. Deep in her heart, she knew she would keep this little girl safe, no matter what it took. She would do so with Adam; she had done so with Todd. With that thought lingering throughout her heart, she fell into a comforting nap.

CHAPTER 14

WHY

Back in Heaven, Todd sat on a cloud wall as Joe appeared next to him. Throughout the day, he had been careful to stay the correct distance from his mom. He felt an urgency and calm coming from her so far. He felt deep sadness from his dad. It had been painful for him to see his dad so broken, head hanging down at the bar. He appreciated Joe's humor as the elder encouraged his dad to talk about his feelings. In that way, he realized now, he and Adam were different from his dad. They had learned to share their feelings, no matter how brief, no matter how angry. His mom had coaxed it out of both of them. Openness and honesty. His dad was honest as well. Always encouraged the truth. But now Todd realized that his father could not express the one truth that was killing his spirit. Todd thought about this afternoon. He had been sitting in the middle of the backseat and Haley was just chattering away. He had seen his mother looking in the rearview mirror, raising her eyebrows as Haley was speaking. He froze. For a moment, he thought for sure his mother had seen him.

"Do you think she saw me?" Todd asked. "I touched her hair when I tried to get some fries."

He felt a gentle push on his arm as Joe replied, "She felt it, I'm sure. She thought it was me. I had to look away or she would have slugged me."

Todd smiled at his words. 'No, she wouldn't."

He sighed, slumping his shoulders.

"We were going to move out, just before." He glanced at Joe. "She asked me if I wanted to come or stay with dad." His eyes warmed with the memory. "She knew I would say yes."

He started swirling with the clouds at his feet.

"I actually found a place, right behind the grocery store where I worked that early shift. I could have walked. I could have slept in a bit longer too." He chuckled at his thought.

"I mean I loved my dad. But it was really hard for me to stay sober when he was drinking. If he was drinking, I'd ask mom if she minded if I had a beer. I always waited to see if he was going to drink. I mean...if he couldn't do it, how could I?"

They sat looking through the clouds at his house below.

"I told her we knew," he whispered.

Silence.

Todd shrugged. "I told her Adam and I knew that she was the one who kept our family together. He was a great dad. He did everything with us. He coached us, played ball with us. Took us to movies and took us for rides. Just for an adventure." He glanced at Joe and sighed. "You know, we would hide when he would come home from work. He'd always say, 'where are those guys?'"

Todd smiled, wistfully. "Adam would get mad at me because I'd go to the same spot every time. The corner inside his closet." He glanced at Joe again, smiling. "Adam would tell me to change spots because dad would always find me." He chuckled. "I was little. He always found me first. Adam was always the hard one to find. He always chose different spots." Todd basked in the familiar happiness of his childhood.

"He used to take us both in his arms and pretend he was the Incredible Hulk. We loved that."

Melancholy crept in as he remembered life on Earth as a little boy, then as a young man. All the happiness and peace he had felt the past few weeks dissipated as he looked down on his home.

"I just don't know why..." His words were a confused whisper.

"Why your dad doesn't stop drinking?"

Todd glanced at the man next to him, who reminded him more and more of his father, before his total submission to alcoholism.

"No," his voice broke. "Why I had to die."

Silence.

The Scribe cleared his throat and started to explain.

"I watched your whole story, Todd, on the sky screen," The Scribe said. "The moment *it* happened, the Big Guy wanted me to understand you so I could help you adjust. I enjoyed watching you grow. I never had siblings, so I loved seeing you and Adam growing up. You two were good brothers. You were good to each other. Your heart was giving out. It was your time. You had a good life. Once up here, it was important that you share your life with all the other angels here who didn't have that kind of love.

Todd nodded, listening.

"He'll get it," Scribs continued, nodding towards his father. "You did."

"Yeah, but only because I wanted to get my driver's license back and I saw how my dad's drinking was hurting mom."

He paused. "You know what she said to me, when she picked me up from work that day?" He saw Joe hang his head and wipe an eye.

"I came out after work and got into the car and she was looking at me with this smile on her face." Todd swallowed, remembering. "I was worried that I wasn't where my friends were in life. I was proud of them, of course. She reminded me of the time when she had told me that I had at least two years to catch up with my friends. I was disappointed in myself and depressed because I wasn't where I wanted to be. She said I just had to give it more time."

Todd looked down and saw his mother getting Haley ready for Adam to arrive. He felt something soft and wet on his face.

He turned to Joe, who wore an easy, sad smile.

"That day, she told me that not only had I made up for those years, but that I was a wonderful, strong twenty-six-year-old who was wise beyond my years. She told me she was very proud of me."

Todd straightened his shoulders and once again looked at Joe.

"She hugged me and she told me that."

Todd saw a longing look in Joe's eyes.

"Well, I think your mom is a pretty special lady. I had someone like your mom once. It was a long time ago."

Todd looked at Joe and nodded. Here was someone who seemed to find peace and harmony in his life up here.

Joe cleared his throat.

"And to answer your question of why you had to die, well, it was just your time. From where I see, you should have died in that car accident. I mean, you were in pretty bad shape. You just missed severing your cervical spine and that hematoma. You had brain surgery twice in three weeks. Sheesh! You should have seen your car." Todd heard the respect in his voice as he continued. "You could have given up. No one would have blamed you if you just got tired of trying." Joe took a deep breath, then continued. "But you didn't."

"I wanted to a few times. I didn't think I would get better. Everything hurt so much. I shook, I couldn't think quickly. I felt like a zombie." He glanced at Joe with a coy smile. "I looked like one, too, with my neck brace and all. I just wanted everything to go away." Todd shrugged and then smiled. "Mom kept telling me I would get better. She wouldn't let me give up." He looked sincerely at Joe. "I just believed her."

Joe sighed loudly. He stood, and seemed to float upon the clouds.

"Well, we'd better get going," he said. "I found all the children. They've chosen their families, you know. So, here's the plan. Your friends are going to start calling Adam. By this time, they've all taken care of the children they found. They have seen the television reports and the children mentioned you. Your friends are worried about you and Haley."

Todd noticed a look in Joe's eyes that expressed something even more than his words.

"You've got some pretty great friends, and family. Not one of them panicked. Each family welcomed the child, deciding on their own what to do. Adam's on his way. He's told everyone to bring the children to your house so we can figure this out."

Todd followed Joe's gaze down to earth. They saw news vans already turning down the long driveway towards his home. The Scribe sighed long and hard, looking at Todd with a determined smile.

"Well, we'd better get going. It's gonna start to get real messy real soon."

He raised his eyes upward, and with a chuckle, he said, "I hope those people down there have a sense of humor."

With a wisp, they were gone.

They landed in the woods behind Todd's house. A slight breeze rustled the leaves and Todd inhaled deeply, remembering the smell of fires burning in fireplaces as late afternoon started to create small shadows. He heard a deep inhale and looked over at Joe. The older angel was standing with his hands folded behind his back, head up, eyes closed. A peaceful smile spread across his face.

"Don't you just love the fall." he said, breathing deeply. "Ah, it's times like this that I really miss *my* life!" He winked at Todd and started to walk, but stopped at the sound of leaves crunching below. A glimpse of sadness spread over the old angel's face when he looked back at Todd. "Ah...life. Ya just gotta love it. *All* of it."

Todd followed behind as Joe walked carefully to the side of the house, peeking around the corner of the chimney at the commotion in the driveway. Television cameras were set up and people began speaking into their earphones. It was just in time for the first evening news of the day.

"Your brother should be here any minute," Joe warned. "Remember, stay back and don't get too close. His emotions will draw you in. No matter what happens, stay back, OK?" Todd nodded and remained behind the chimney. Then he remembered he could not be seen by people on Earth. He moved closer to the driveway, leaning against the side of the garage and watched as more vans pulled down the long driveway. Curious neighbors began to gather outside.

Joe moved towards the driveway and his appearance immediately changed. He was no longer wearing the flannel shirt and khaki pants, but a tailored black suit. His back was straight, his hair combed back and he was adjusting a white collar around his neck. He winked back at Todd, and when he turned, Todd noticed the large silver cross he wore around his neck. A bible appeared in Joe's hand and just as quickly it disappeared. Todd smiled as Joe shrugged his shoulders and moved towards the growing crowd. No one seemed to notice or question that this man just appeared out of nowhere.

Todd felt an immense pull, as if the undertow of a large wave was pushing him first forward, then backwards, making him dizzy. That's when he noticed his brother's SUV up on the road, and Adam and Lindsay were walking down the driveway. There was a little boy between them, holding their hands.

"Father, Father. What are you doing here? Do you know anything about the missing children?" Joe ignored the gaggle of voices yelling above one another to get their questions heard first. He walked up to Adam, arm outstretched.

Todd watched as The Scribe spoke quietly to his brother. Lindsay was looking around at all the people, her mouth opened in awe at the scene. She looked up with a smile, and gave a small wave to someone at the window. Todd followed her eyes to see Haley peeking out the bedroom window, waving back. When she saw him, a brilliant smile caressed her face and her wave became urgent. She tried to open the window. He stepped back to the side of the garage so she couldn't see him anymore.

After exchanging a few words, Adam nodded and started up the walkway to the front door. He glanced towards Todd and for a moment Todd felt that tremendous pull of yearning. He quickly stepped back again, resting against the side of the house.

He was beginning to understand the unique dimension they were in, and was learning the distance he needed to keep from certain people. It wasn't Earth itself that beckoned him. It was the pull of each of the ones he loved. It's funny, but he had realized yesterday at the bar that he could sit right next to his dad and not feel anything at all. Joe explained that it was because his dad didn't believe. His father was still so deep in mourning and booze and paranormal thinking that he could not allow himself to feel the blending of life and spirit. He felt nothing from his father and his father could not feel his presence at all. He blinked back a tear of frustration.

Suddenly Todd heard a voice in the crowd, commanding attention.

"Hey everyone! I have news about all those children!!" Todd leaned around the chimney to see Joe standing on his front porch. His right arm was up in the air, waving in rhythm. Todd smiled, shaking his head.

The crowd gathered around with reporters whispering into earphones and the air filled with the clicking of technology as cameras and cell phones urgently captured the moment.

Lindsay moved towards Adam, gently leading the boy, holding his hand.

Joe spoke, puffing out his chest, trying to sound authentic.

"Everyone wants to know what is happening here in this quaint town of..." he paused for a moment, looking up to the sky.

"Woodridge Lake. I get that. I'm a bit confused myself. There are government officials meeting at St. Margret's Church in Manassas, getting ready to have a press conference any minute. You'll find out much more than I... or we even know."

Joe gestured towards the house and Adam.

"Who are you?" "Are you a priest" "Are these the real missing children? We thought they were dead." "Are they going to be reunited with their families?"

"Did this lady kidnap them?" "How did she do it?"

Ignoring their questions, Joe held out his arms in a scooting manner, like a preacher encouraging his flock. "Go quickly now. You know, whoever gets there first will have the headline story!"

Resting against the side of the garage, Todd watched as news crews, reporters, neighbors and strangers began rushing up the driveway. Only one person lingered in front of the house, hands folded in hope. It was their neighbor, Dana.

"Adam," she said, quietly. "I know what's going on. It's a miracle. A Christmas Miracle."

Adam stepped off the porch and walked the short distance to where Dana stood.

"Tell your mom that I know who these children are and I'm here for her."

Adam accepted the card she was holding and nodded.

From beside the house, Todd stepped onto the driveway, moving towards them, wanting to see the card, but caught Joe's warning glance.

"Thank you, Ms. Reid. I don't know what's going on. But I'll tell her." Adam turned back to the house, holding the card she had given him.

"They're angels." Adam turned back towards her. Dana was smiling, nervously. "What else could they be?"

She turned and walked back towards her house. Adam glanced down at the card in his hand.

It showed both Mary and Joseph, and in the center was a baby Jesus. It read, *The Carmelite Prayer.*

Looking up at the now empty driveway, the echo of the crowd dissipating in the distance, Todd watched as the older angel joined Adam on the front porch of his home.

"God, ya gotta love people, especially the press," he said, pulling his hands through his hair. "So, we're good? You made the calls?

His eyebrows furrowed as he glanced at Todd, then peeked over Adam's shoulder to glance at the card.

"Oh, that's my favorite prayer of almost all time!" Joe said, smiling. He bent down to look at the little boy standing protectively in front of Lindsay.

"Hey, Stephen. How you doing? All right?"

Stephen smiled sadly as he leaned shyly into Lindsay's legs.

"I have to go back, don't I?"

"Yeah, Little Buddy. But it's going to be all right."

Todd had moved a bit closer to hear better. The little boy's eyes opened widely, and his mouth gaped. Todd put his finger to his lips as he smiled and Joe distracted them all by saying, "Well, we better go in and get started. We don't have much time and Lieutenant Matthews is going to be here soon with kind of bad news."

Adam opened the front door and Lindsay led the little boy inside. Todd watched as Joe grabbed Adam's arm, to stop him before going inside.

"Hey, Adam. Am I dressed okay? I mean, should I wear something else as we get all the other children? I don't want to get arrested for faking a priest."

Todd watched Adam's face as Joe suddenly was wearing the plaid flannel shirt, khaki pants, and black converse shoes he'd been wearing before. Even though he'd spent over two days on Earth, his clothes seemed fresh and clean. But the hair, and the scruffy beard--maybe those could go.

"Oh, yeah," Joe agreed. He glanced at Adam's startled look and smiled. "I guess I should have told you to shut your eyes."

In a blink, Joe's beard was trimmed to match that of Adam, and his hair was smartly combed back. Eyes wide, Adam shook his head and looked at Lindsay.

"Oh, my God." Lindsay had been waiting for Adam inside the door. Her face was pale and she leaned into Adam's back, looking over his shoulder, fear replacing awe.

"Did he just…"

"Hey, let's get inside and get this thing done. It will all make sense in a bit."

"You *are* an angel…" Lindsay's voice trailed softly.

Todd watched as Adam put his arm around his wife and led the three of them into the house. Joe paused, glancing at Adam, eyebrows raised. "How do I look?"

Adam laughed awkwardly. "You kind of look like my Uncle Chuck."

Joe flashed him a wide grin and winked as he stepped inside the doorway.

"Thank you. I want to look my best for Alice."

He poked his head back out to look at Todd. "I'm *kidding*, Todd! Sheesh!"

With those words, the door closed and Todd stood on the front porch of his home, looking around at the soft snow that was beginning to freeze on the front lawn.

Oh, how he missed this life on Earth. With a deep sigh, he shrugged his shoulders, hanging his head. He didn't like this feeling of sorrow, but he knew that this place was no longer where he belonged.

Something brown caught his eye and he looked at the corner of the brick steps. The little toad had hopped up and was taking its usual place as the centaur, protecting the house and everyone inside.

In a split second, Todd realized why it was there and why he was suddenly filled with a sense of dread. There was an increasing commotion coming from inside his house. He heard his father yelling, and Haley was crying. Filled with a renewed sense of purpose, he entered his home and sat on the kitchen counter, watching and waiting for the events to unfold.

CHAPTER 15

MIRACLES

Alice woke at the sound of the alarm, an anxious flutter dancing its way through her body. She looked down at the little girl who was stirring next to her. Two days ago, this little girl just showed up, asking her to be her mommy. Yesterday morning, it was actually *snowing* children on her front lawn. That scene they all witnessed was unbelievable. Inexplicable; undeniably a miracle. She thought about taking something for her anxiety and sighed. Just as a drink wouldn't solve this situation, no anxiety medication would make this any less bewildering.

Alice felt a hand touch her face and she looked down at Haley's sleepy face.

"Mommy, did you like that man we met this morning?"

"Yes, I did. How do you know him?"

Haley's arms wrapped around her neck, and she smelled the sweetness of honeysuckle that surrounded the little girl since that first day.

"Well..." Haley tried not to lie. "I know him from- where I was before I came here!"

Haley bounced off the bed and went to look out the window. Alice followed and together they watched as Lt. Matthew's black

SUV pulled down the driveway. Behind him followed a caravan of news trucks and vans. Alice scrambled to change into sweatpants and sweater before going down to open the front door. She let Haley stay in her pajamas, but when she glanced back at her, the little girl was wearing her yellow dress with the pink bow, crisp and perfect.

Haley took her hand and looked up at Alice with wide, earnest eyes.

"Well, I guess now you know!" Haley said, happily.

Lieutenant Matthews stood in the center of the stoop, ignoring the gathering crowd.

"There's been a change since I talked with you yesterday," he was saying. "May I come in?"

Alice moved aside to let him in the foyer. Her heart began to pound hard as she saw the sad smile he gave Haley as he stooped to say hello.

Alice walked with Matthews as Haley tiptoed into the family room, peeking over the railing to see if Ben was still asleep. With sparkling eyes, she looked at Alice when she saw the channel was still on her favorite cartoon.

"I like to splash in muddy puddles!" her voice mimicked the characters.

"Would you like some coffee?" Alice offered, but before he could answer she heard a soft whimper coming from Haley.

"Daddy, don't. I don't want to watch this," she whispered to Ben.

"Excuse me a moment," Alice said as she moved into the family room and reached for the remote. "Ben, she was watching that show..." Her voice trailed as she watched Haley slowly move towards the television.

"Mommy. That's me, again! Why am I always on the TV?

Alice dropped the remote and lowered herself onto the edge of the recliner, her eyes widening at the images on the screen.

Matthews touched her shoulder and she glanced at his worried look.

"This is what has happened overnight."

Transfixed, she watched as a couple were insisting to the interviewer that the Thomas family had taken their little girl and should be arrested immediately for kidnapping. A picture of Haley flashed in the corner of the screen. Haley Jenson had been missing since this past September, and they had never stopped searching for her, even after the police said there was nothing more they could do. They were angry because they became the first and only suspects. They wanted their little girl home. Talking to the camera, they informed the audience that they were consulting a lawyer about the way they were treated by the authorities and talked directly to the camera.

"Haley, sweetheart. We love you and no matter what they did to you, you are welcomed home. We want you home, sweetie."

Alice swallowed the anger that welled up inside at their attempt to sound sincere. She reached for the remote and turned to the detective in disbelief as she turned off the TV. She reached down to stroke Haley's hair and the little girl grabbed both her hands, her eyes moist and wide.

"They're lying. They know they are. Why do they want me back when they were so mean to me!"

Swallowing to quell her growing fear, Alice turned to Lt. Matthews as she stood.

"What's going on? What was that on the news?"

Lt. Matthews shifted in his stance and sighed heavily.

"The FBI are involved as well as The Center for Missing Children. This all started once the children started showing up here yesterday. It's been all over the news."

Alice noticed he was choosing his words carefully.

"Each parent has been the center of suspicion, especially these parents who claim that Haley is their daughter. They want her back. All the other parents who recognize their children have been calling. They are joining together with a group of lawyers who are defending that they have been wrongfully accused when their children were actually kidnapped by...you."

Alice looked at him, eyes wide, dumbfounded by the insinuation that she had somehow kidnapped all these children. Her heart fluttered as her mind confirmed what she had sensed all along. Days ago, she'd accepted that whoever Haley was, at this moment in time, she was supposed to be here, right now. With her.

"But you saw what we all saw," she said quietly. He looked at her nodding, then shrugged his shoulders.

"I really don't understand what I saw."

Ben wobbled to sit up straight, glaring at Alice through swollen, bloodshot eyes.

"Now I get all this! Did you *kidnap* this little girl, Alice? Is that how she got here? Is that what makes you feel good? She's *replacing* Todd?"

Alice stared at her husband, allowing her resentments to rise, pushing past all the tolerance she had tried to have over the past several weeks. She took a step forward, forgetting everyone else in the room. She was heartbroken and she was angry.

"Are you kidding me?" She said, trying to keep her voice steady. She shrugged at the detective, unwilling to apologize. "Are you kidding me? After you calling all our friends when you're drunk as a skunk and telling them I was an alien dressed in a female's body and that I was trying to collect bodies for experiments? Are you kidding me? You were here! You were here when she came to us. Did you forget that?"

Her face was flushed and she felt dizzy and betrayed. She had tolerated his behavior and his delusional thinking because he was suffering and grieving as much as she was. She had stayed here, spending only nights at her brother's house because as much as she wanted to stay sober, she needed Ben as much as he needed her to get through the most devastating time of their lives.

Now he had gone too far. Alice stood in front of him, hands on hips as Ben stood on wobbly legs, swaying to keep himself steady.

"You are not a good person," he said, belching. "It's your fault our son died." He looked at her with a semblance of pride. "There! I finally said it. You're the reason he died. You probably gave him something...one of your pills or something." He had moved to the doorway of the garage, leaning his arms against the side.

Alice was stunned at his words and the anger swelled inside. She looked at Lt. Matthews and then back at Ben.

"Now, Mr. Thomas. Settle down. You know that didn't happen. It was his heart. He had an enlarged heart and heart disease no one knew about. Do you remember?"

In an instant, Ben was sobbing, shaking his head and hugging the wall.

"I have to get out of here. I don't know what's going on any-more. You're no one I want to be around. You're a witch! Both boys always loved you more than me! Even this little girl would rather be with you. You think you're so perfect because you were able to stop drinking and I can't! You turned them against me! "

"That's not true at all and you know that!"

A voice boomed behind them and Alice turned to see Adam and Lindsay standing just inside the kitchen. The new friend, Joe, was peeking out from behind Adam.

"It's your drinking! It's always been your drinking! No one wants to be around you when you're drinking, so don't blame mom!"

Alice heard the crack in her son's voice as he said what he had tried to say for many years. Her heart ached that the one thing she could not protect her sons from was the devastation of seeing their father's alcoholism. He was a good father, a great provider, actively involved in their family. But he would never acknowledge that, when he was in a delusional alcohol driven stupor, his behavior and his words hurt everyone he loved.

"I don't want to be here anymore." Ben slumped against the wall, sobbing.

"Then why don't you just go! Leave! You're making everyone miserable!"

The room was stunned with silence. Alice could hear her heart pumping in her ears. The grandfather clock in the other room ticked loudly.

"Daddy, please don't go!"

Haley's voice echoed quietly in the stormy silence.

"You love mommy. You love me. Why are you so mad?"

"Ben, please stop. Look at Haley." Alice said, calmer now, knowing that anything she said would only escalate the situation. She felt Adam's hands touching her shoulders and she glanced back to see Joe peeking around Lindsay. A smile tugged at the corner of her mouth to see him trying to hide, then she turned again to the scene in front of her. Ben slumped to the floor, eyes wide, trying to focus.

Haley was pressed against the wall, arms by her side, tears streaming down her cheeks. Her sobs echoed in the evening air. She looked past Alice towards the kitchen counter. Alice turned to look at the kitchen counter, following Haley's eyes.

"I want to go back with you, Todd! I don't want to go back to those mean people. They hurt me! And it's too angry here. I want to go home with you!" Her eyes darted between the counter and Joe. "Please!"

Alice put her hand to her heart when she heard her son's name. She saw a flash of light, a quick reflection of something she instantly recognized but couldn't fathom. Memories of a hand held in sleep, of whispers in her ear when her heart was breaking suddenly became all too real.

When she heard the little girl call out her son's name, she knew. Blinking back the logic that said this could not be possible, *she knew*. What was happening was real and unbelievable and magical. Todd was here. Now.

She turned back to look at Haley but what she saw made her jaw drop. Tears welled in her eyes.

The sweet little girl with the yellow dress and bouncing white curls was floating upwards, ever slowly, seeming to evaporate in the air until just her eyes and her hair could be seen.

"Haley, no! Ben!."

As if clarity had struck Ben sober, he was on his knees, trying to stand up. He looked at Haley, and his arms dropped to his side.

"I'm sorry, Haley. I'm so sorry! I didn't mean any of it. I miss my son so much. I don't know how to go on without him." His head dropped to his chest and he reached out for Alice. She took his hand and looked up at Haley.

"I'm sorry, too, Haley. Grownups sometimes get mad and say mean things. But we still love each other. Please don't go."

Haley glanced at the counter and then at Joe, who was now standing beside Adam, arms crossed, faking a stern look.

"Oh, all right..." Haley sighed. "But I will NOT go back to those people!"

Slowly, Haley drifted back down to the floor, a halo of light shining behind her.

Alice blinked, for in that moment, she thought she glimpsed a veil of white feathers gently swaying in the light behind Haley.

"Hey, Haley...," said a small voice, and the little boy who came with Adam stepped forward. Joe moved behind him, holding his shoulders. A smile spread across her face as she stepped towards the little boy.

"Hey, Stephen! Did you come to play?" Haley's face brightened.

"Actually, we have to go back to Heaven. It's getting 'complicated'." The little boy looked up at Joe.

"Geez, you humans," Joe grumbled, eyeing Matthews. "You make *everything* so complicated. Everything's going to be all right. We found out where all the children are and Adam here already called them. Everyone's on their way.

"And just how did you do that so quickly?" Matthews raised an eyebrow.

Alice smiled as Joe rolled his eyes and said as politely as he could. "Have you noticed everything that's happened in the last two days? I know you're a pretty sharp guy. Aced the Lieutenant test and all..."

Joe stooped before Haley, resting his arms on his bent legs.

"Am I in trouble?" she asked, innocently.

"Hmmm, kind of...just a little bit but nothing that can't be fixed." He smiled at her. "You see, in a few minutes all your friends that came here yesterday will join us and then all of you have to go back to Heaven."

"Excuse me," Matthews stepped towards Joe. "Just who *are* you?"

"I'm a friend of the family," Joe replied easily and cocked an eyebrow. "You?"

"You obviously know who I am. Haley, this little boy and all the other children, need to go back to their parents."

"Why?" Alice heard a firmness in Joe's voice she hadn't heard before. He stepped closer to the lieutenant. "They reported them *missing*. Most of those parents know what happened to their children." Joe widened his arms, exasperated. "Don't you get anything that's happened here today? Did you just see that little girl like almost disappear and then come back? Don't you have even a smidgen of who they might be? Of what's going on here?"

Matthews stood quietly, shoulders slumped in resolve.

"It doesn't matter what I think," he said, quietly. "These children are missing and now they are here and their parents want them back. What am I supposed to do?"

"Uh, let me see." Joe feigned rubbing his chin. "How about... *your job?*"

"I had nothing to do with any of this."

"Yeah, yeah. I know. I'm not blaming you, or anyone else. All I'm saying is now that you know, what you saw here, maybe you could help the authorities find these children. Let them go in peace."

"How do I do that? There's no proof, no evidence."

"Stephen," Adam spoke, looking down at the little boy who had showed up in his car last night. "Can you tell the detective what you told Lindsay and me this morning?"

"My daddy's girlfriend took me from school on Science Day." Stephen glanced at Joe, who nodded sadly. "I'm up in the marsh, north of where we live. She just left me there. I got lost and fell into the deep end of the marsh. I couldn't get out. I'm still there."

Matthews reluctantly took out a little black notebook, flipped it open and started writing.

"What is your name?"

"Stephen Hatcher...from Seattle."

Lt. Matthews clicked on his cellphone. He looked up, surprised. "That was two years ago."

He bent down in front of Haley.

"So, Haley. Tell me what you know about your parents."

"They were really mean to me." She leaned in to whisper in his ear. "They let me die," she said, quietly.

Alice nodded as Lieutenant Matthews cast her a pointed look.

"Well, they never found her," he said to Alice.

"Did anyone really look?"

Alice remembered something Haley had told her when she had first appeared. She bent down next to Matthews, and gently prodded. "Haley. The ring, and your bunny."

Haley nodded eagerly. "I *never* go anywhere without my bunny. And my ring was on my finger. And I had a little brace on my leg to help me walk 'cause I had cancer when I was little." She looked up at Alice innocently. "I'm in the woodpile."

Alice felt the sudden sadness that overwhelmed this little girl, blinking back her own tears at Haley's courage to state it so simply.

Joe cleared his throat. "Well, is that enough to consider checking that woodpile again? Maybe find her ring, and her brace, and her..." he winked at Haley, trying to lighten up the conversation."... and her bunny?"

Matthews looked at everyone in disbelief.

"To be honest, I don't know how I am going to explain any of this, but I saw what I saw." He glanced at Joe. "And yeah, I know what I know."

Ben moved towards the kitchen, towards Adam.

They heard sounds coming from outside the house.

"I think we have company," Joe said. "I can give you all the names of these children and tell you everything." He turned to the detective. "But we need to do it fast."

"I want you to come with me to make this report. We will need your help."

Joe raised an eyebrow to the detective, hiding a smile.

"Really? Have you thought about who *I am?*"

"You're not God, I don't think." Matthews hesitated foolishly, shrugging his shoulders.

"Nah. The Big Guy is busy watching over the universe. So, he sends messengers like me, well in today's world." He chuckled sadly. "God knows how someone else would be treated if HE came back today." Joe raised his eyes upward, mouthing, 'Thank you!' "I just gave you the list of children, their parents and where they live. Everything you need to bring these children peace."

Matthews glanced down at his notepad and noticed it was nicely organized, page by page, of names and addresses and other information. He looked up at Joe, shaking his head.

The doorbell chimed as Alice walked with Matthews to the door.

"Thank you for believing in all this," she said, reaching to shake his hand. She saw him glance around.

"What's not to believe? Children falling like snow on the ground. A little girl evaporating. And, I swear, I saw her wings."

He moved towards the door, then turned back to face everyone.

"Take care, everyone and good luck!" Haley ran to him, hugging his legs. He reached down to touch her hair. "You especially, little one. No one's taking you back anywhere. You belong where you are."

With that, he opened the door, taking one more look at Joe before he left.

"And if you are who I think you are, I hope you will watch out for me."

Alice smiled as Joe winked. "Yeah, yeah. Well, I won't be seeing you for a very long time."

Lt. Matthews stepped through the opened door, brushing past the group of friends walking up to the door, holding the hands of children.

As the guests entered the foyer, the children started hugging each other, smiling and laughing. Haley moved through the group to stand over near the kitchen window. Alice blinked back tears as she saw the little girl lean forward as if whispering in someone's ear. Then she gave an imaginary hug, looking up towards the ceiling where no one was, a smile playing across her lips.

Alice swallowed as Haley looked at her with wonder in her eyes. The little girl came towards her, taking her hand and Joe ushered everyone else into the family room.

Alice bent her head as Haley tiptoed to whisper something in her ear.

She held the little girl tightly, embracing the smell of honeysuckle; memorizing the touch of soft curls against her cheek. Alice closed her eyes as Haley stepped back. She felt little hands on each side of her cheeks.

"You are the best mommy ever."

With a skip and a hop, Haley went to join the others in the family room.

Touching her cheeks, Alice embraced the words Haley had whispered in her ear. Tears streamed down her cheeks as the miracle of what had happened the past two days sunk in. Her heart swelled with pride and understanding. Todd was here. He was helping. Haley came down to Earth because of all the wonderful stories Todd had been sharing with them in Heaven.

Alice stood and saw Joe standing next to her, a gentle look of knowing on his face.

"I know, I know," he said, his voice choking a little. "But everyone is waiting for us, and..." he offered her a kind grin. "You look worse than I do."

Joe offered her a handkerchief, and Alice blew her nose. Without thinking, she handed it back to Joe. For once, Joe wasn't crude. He tucked the handkerchief into his pocket, patting it.

She waited for a moment, taking in a deep breath.

"I know you're here, Todd. I can feel you. I always do. I miss you so much."

She crossed in front of Joe as she went to face the dozen or so family and friends and the children who came with them. She entered the room, smiling warmly as she met each face, eagerly waiting for some explanation of what was happening and where things would go from here.

It would be well into the night before anyone could fully absorb the miracle of what had occurred; before anyone could fully accept what was best for the children.

All of the little ones needed to return to Heaven.

CHAPTER 16

ALL THE LITTLE CHILDREN NEED TO COME HOME

Finding himself suddenly standing in the kitchen he knew so well, Todd felt a tingling sensation that warned him that Earth's power and the love of his mother was drawing him in. He squeezed his eyes tightly, fighting the pull as he heard her speak softly to Haley. He concentrated on her voice, and then, through a mist of memories, he saw himself laying on the floor of his bedroom again, so many weeks ago. He felt himself leaving his body. At that time, he was so afraid. He remembered the last words his mom had whispered in his ear that day as she kissed the top of his head. The kiss was a soft whisper in his soul.

"I love you, Todd. "

The next moment he was back in the kitchen with his mom standing right beside him, looking out the window. His heart pounded with the desire to reach out and touch her. Giving in, he tried to touch her shoulder, to tell her that yes, he was here. He'd come back to her.

But before he could make contact, she'd turned towards the family room. He felt her alarm as she set her eyes on the TV. Dropping his hand to his side, he closed his eyes again, relishing in the memories of all that had happened in his home, knowing that, although it was against the rules, he wanted to hug his mom one last time.

His reminiscing stopped just as quickly as it had started. He heard Haley sobbing. Looking towards the TV, he saw the parents being interviewed on a morning news show. He watched his father sit up and belch. Todd flinched.

He heard Haley call his name, saying that she wanted to stay with his mommy. She looked right at him. By now, he realized that angels in human form could still see other angels.

Nodding quickly, he put his finger to his lips, but not before his mother looked right at him. He caught her gaze, and even though he knew she couldn't see him, he smiled at her and tried to let her know things would be all right. He knew they would be, because Joe told him so. Just as his mom had told him years before that he would recover from his accident, and that he would be all right.

For a moment, he thought she saw him. Her eyes brightened when she glanced his way. But then she turned back to the TV, where Haley's parents were asking for the Thomas' to be immediately arrested for kidnapping their daughter.

Ben wobbled to sit up straight, glaring at Alice through swollen eyes.

"Now I get all this! Did you *kidnap* this little girl? Is that how she got here?"

"Are you kidding me?"

What Todd saw was something he recognized instantly when his mother had had enough and was not going to back down. She'd lift her chin, cross her arms, look directly into anyone's face, and her voice would be eerily calm. When they would see this, both he and Adam knew - Mama Bear was here. He was still amazed that while keeping her voice quiet, her words could pierce the air, making her point perfectly clear. He almost felt sorry for his father as the argument escalated into hurtful words.

His father had gone too far.

Ben moved into the laundry room, reaching for his coat, grabbing the keys to his car.

"I have to get out of here. I don't what's going on anymore. Even Haley doesn't like me! You turned everyone against me!"

From behind him, Todd heard a beloved voice.

"That's not true at all and you know that!" Adam was in the kitchen, and Joe was peeking out from behind Lindsay who stood, mouth opened, holding the hand of a little boy.

"Daddy, please don't go!"

Haley's voice echoed quietly in the stormy silence.

"You love mommy. You love me. Why are you so mad?"

Ben slumped down to the floor, his eyes wide, trying to focus.

"I want to go back with you, Todd! I don't want to go back to those mean people. They hurt me! And it's too angry here. I want to go home with you! *Please!*"

Her eyes darted between the counter and Joe.

The room was suddenly silent as everyone looked at Haley. Todd tried to smile when Haley looked right at him, tears welling in her eyes.

"I don't want to go back to those mean people. It's too angry here. I want to go back with you!"

Then, without warning, Haley started to rise, like a slow mist disappearing in the air. She was vanishing in front of their eyes until only a simple outline of her face and her yellow curls remained.

Todd ached for his father as he watched him sobbing. Maybe *now* his father would realize how much his drinking was harming those he loved.

"No, Haley! Don't go! It's me. It's all me. I just miss Todd so much!"

Alice stepped towards Ben, reaching out her hand. He grabbed it, and she stooped next to him, patting his back, looking at Adam.

"Hey, Haley..."

The boy who was holding Lindsay's hand stepped forward, waving at her.

"Hey, Stephen..."

Todd felt the immense emotions of everyone in the room as Haley slowly drifted down to the family room, wiping her tears with her sleeve.

"It's okay, Daddy," she said, moving to stand in front of Ben. "I'll stay."

Matthews opened up his black notebook and started to write down the things the Haley and Stephen told him. He looked up at Joe. "You're going to have to come with me when I make these reports. To validate."

"Uh, no I don't. They are all right there in your little black book." He rolled his eyes.

Matthews flipped open the book and all the pages were filled with writing. His eyes widened, perplexed.

"I'm not sure what just happened, but I think you have company coming and I have some explaining to do. I guess I'm leaving just in time."

Matthews shook Alice's hand and they exchanged easy pleasantries. Todd looked at Joe, and nodded. Todd realized that Joe knew exactly how all this was going to end. As friends and family gathered in the family room, Todd winked at Haley, and mouthed, 'Be right back.'

He took this moment to go up into his bedroom. As he passed by his brother, he flipped him gently on the back of his head, and smiled as Adam reached back to rub the area.

Todd stood in the doorway of the bedroom he had lived in for almost twenty-four of his twenty-six years and stepped inside.

He wanted to feel his life one last time.

He was one and a half when they moved to this new house, with the fresh walls, big rooms and a wonderful back yard. Memories flashed as the walls changed from Forest Green, where he and

Adam helped spongepaint the walls and his crib changed into a little bed for a growing toddler; changed again to a lighter blue for the budding athlete, where posters of Michael Jordan and his own sports trophies graced the walls; until lastly, the muted green again of a young man, coming home from college after the first month of school. He glanced out his bedroom window where he would sit on the ledge sometimes, his feet resting on the roof of the bay window below. He saw himself and his brother playing in the sandbox, catching tadpoles in the creek; his front and back yard was a baseball diamond, a football field, a wonderful hill to sleigh down. He and Adam had friends over and sleep overs and birthday parties and sport parties; his cousins would often spend a weekend over and his world was exactly as it should have been. He sat on his bed, and laid back. He closed his eyes, and allowed himself to absorb the peace that filled the room.

From downstairs, Todd heard the families talking and hugging as they arrived. He knew he didn't have much time. He remembered how he and his mother had spent that last day. They'd sat down at the computer for a couple of games of Family Feud. A few days before, he had visited the Navy recruiting office and took a test. When he finished, the young officer shook his hand and told him he would be a perfect candidate for their program. He had just filled out the application to be a stringer for the Washington Nationals come spring, and just the day before, he had contacted the university where he had dropped out after his junior year to get some information about how he might graduate.

After a few years of struggling to find himself again, he had plans and was looking forward to his future. He made it through with the love and support of his parents, his brother, his family and his friends. The last weeks and months of his life had been the best since his accident. He felt complete and he felt hopeful. He was starting on a new journey where everything he thought he'd lost he now believed he would find again.

Life was good. He realized now that *he had the best last day of his life.*

He had opened the pretzel Twix, remembering to leave the last one in the box. On his way upstairs, he peeked into the Library, where his father was sitting to do taxes. He asked if he wanted to go to a matinee with mom and himself. He remembered his father's smile as he said, "we'll see," and with a smile back he went upstairs.

He stepped into his parents' open door and said goodnight to his mother. His heart swelled with pride and hope and acceptance of where he was in life; he had overcome obstacles that should have been unsurmountable. It was just past midnight when he started to watch an episode of NCIS. He was sitting on the bed, eating the Twix and felt very happy and extremely tired. He laid back on the bed, and closed his eyes. All the heaviness of his body now seemed calm and light.

The next thing he knew, his mother was kneeling over him, holding him, crying out his name. Even though it was his last day on Earth--or maybe because it was--he felt absolute love along with confusion and fear.

A sudden tug pulled him from his reverie, and without warning he was downstairs again. He saw a wealth of friends and family standing around Joe as he explained what had happened in Heaven and why all these little children had shown up on Earth.

Todd saw him shrug his way with a grin on his face.

"I know, I know," Joe said in response to the comments and murmurs from the group. "It doesn't seem fair. They will be able to visit you in your dreams from time to time, so it won't feel like you're missing them. You just won't remember missing them," his voice trailed. "It doesn't really make sense at all, but it's the way it is."

Todd stood watching each family hold their little ones, saying goodbye. Each person was protected from the angst of letting them go by a faith in something greater than what is seen.

One by one, each little angel disappeared up into the safety of Heaven. They were happy that, if only for a day, they were able to feel good about themselves. No one yelled at them. No one blamed them for anything. No one harmed them. They felt the peace that came from a family who cared. They felt deeply loved.

Todd was sitting on the center counter island, smiling at everyone saying goodbyes and he felt safe. Things would be all right once all the angels were back in Heaven. Grandpa Carl would probably be making ice cream, waiting for Joe to join him, most likely feigning anger: "Not again! It's not time for snow yet!"

The little ones passed Todd, winking and laughing as they went by. A few of the older ones mouthed "thank you," and he watched in wonder as they disappeared in a soft, snowy mist through the double doors in the kitchen.

Once the children were gone, Todd watched all the families hugging, smiling, wiping each other's tears, and making promises to keep in touch. Soon, Adam and Lindsay, Haley and his parents were the only ones left. He felt Joe next to him, and he bent his head to listen.

"Ok, Toddo. Your mom knows."

Todd glanced at his mother, who was still holding Haley's hand. Her faced glowed as she watched with absolute amazement at what she knew was a miracle.

"I know you're here," she whispered with a smile. "I can feel you."

With her words, he felt the warm tickle of love from his mother flow into him. He glanced at his brother, who had moved next to his mom and was looking towards the french doors where the children had just traveled. Lindsay joined them as they stood there, feeling both the emptiness and the love. They could hear an occasional giggle or the flapping of eager wings as all the children made their way back home.

Joe reached his hand out to Ben.

"Well," he said, swallowing hard. "You're actually a good man, Ben. Shape up. Take care of this woman." He winked at Todd. "Or I will...I mean up *there*, not down here!"

Joe turned to Adam and Lindsay.

"May you both glow in the happiness of this family. It's a good family." He indicated Ben. "Keep loving him. He's a good guy. He'll come around, once he realizes that he won't find any answers in a bottle of Jack Daniels or Ketel One."

"Todd...Toddo..." Todd listened as Adam's voice cracked with sadness. "Be happy, Bro."

Todd looked at Joe, who shrugged his shoulders.

"Oh, all right. You can't do it in human form, but they can see you when you take Haley's hand."

His dad picked up the little girl and held her, tears streaming down his face. Holding his face between her hands, she kissed the top of his nose. She gave Adam a high five and a kiss, and hugged Lindsay, nestling against her legs. Lindsay looked down at the little girl, stroking her hair as she mouthed, "See you around."

Turning to Alice she reached up to hug her tightly.

"I love you, mommy. I always will. I won't ever forget you. You are my best friend ever!"

Haley turned to Todd, with her eyes sparkling, and reached for his outstretched hand. With a quick sidestep, she was out of his grasp and he felt the familiar touch of his mother. Although she couldn't really see his human form, the look of pure joy on her face told him she knew.

"Hey," he said, looking at her, fighting the sadness that started to creep in.

"Hey," she replied. "I miss you so much." She reached to stroke his cheek, as she had done so many times in his life.

He felt the electricity of the love she had for him, and held on to her touch as long as he could.

"I wasn't ready to go, and I miss you all. Thank you for always believing in me. Thank you."

Blinking back tears of both joy and sadness, he felt the tug of Heaven gently reaching for him. But she felt him. She heard him. She knew he was there right in front of her.

With the light from the rising moon flowing through the kitchen window, Todd felt the heaviness give way to extreme love. He watched as Joe turned towards his mom, reaching for her hand that was still outstretched.

"It has been a pleasure," Joe sighed, wistfully. "Another place, another time..."

Joe leaned in and pecked her cheek, winking at Ben all the while.

Todd held Haley's hand, and Joe took her other one.

With one last glimpse of his family, Todd found himself back up among the clouds, the moon shining against the deepening twilight below.

Haley looked sadly at Todd and Joe, and tried to smile, tried to understand.

"I had fun, Todd," she said. Todd looked at Joe, who nodded knowingly.

"Well, kiddo, you know sometimes angels do get another chance," he said. Then, turning, he yelled out, "Hey, now wait just a minute, Grandpa Carl. It's not time to snow again!"

Todd smiled as Joe rolled his eyes towards him.

"Jeez, he's a funny guy, your grandpa. I can see why your mom chose your dad. They're both pretty good men."

With those words, Joe joined The Elders as they gathered to greet the little angels with welcoming hugs and fluffy ice cream.

Todd looked down at Haley, who was smiling again.

"You going to be all right?" he asked her, taking her hand.

Her yellow curls bobbed up and down.

"If I ever go back to Earth again," she said to Todd as she skipped ahead of him. "I hope I find your toad. I think he will miss me, even though I couldn't pet him."

Todd glanced one last time down to Earth, where the darkness enveloped the cold December night.

He smiled, knowing that his family and their world would eventually be all right. Taking Haley's hand, he took one last glance down below, and then joined the others in Heaven as the gentle nightfall embraced his forever home.

CHAPTER 17

BELIEVE

Alice lay in bed, blinking several times, wondering if she would ever stop counting the days since Todd died. It had been weeks since the world as she knew it ended. Today was day forty-four. Each night as she fell asleep, it was on a damp pillow. Every morning, she remembered, and she blinked back the tears that welled up in an attempt to relieve her grieving heart. Kleenex became her best friend, and she reached for a tissue, allowing the alarm that she set every day to ease into a ten-minute snooze.

Human nature instilled a reset button for everyone. She remembered reading that somewhere. Of course, that was for her addiction; it simply meant that one could change, accept, forgive. She knew there could never be a reset button for the loss of her son. There was no humanly way she could ever reset her life back to a time before she lost Todd. The world was going to continue with or without her. She had read about a mother whose grief was so deep, she had opted to have the memories removed so she could try to live her life without always trying to die. Alice understood that grief so well. That deep vast empty hole in the middle of your heart and mind that will always be there.

Yet, Alice could only think of her other son, Adam, needing to keep him sharply in her mind. She was learning that, by choosing to live each day, and not give in to the tremendous anguish of her heart, at some point she would learn to laugh again, find joy in little things, and to bring the spirit of Todd with her into every single day.

She could try. She could learn.

But for now, she turned off the alarm, dropped a leg out from under the covers, turned on the TV, and waited until the wiggling of her legs encouraged the rest of her body to wake up. Before she knew it, she was out of bed, walking downstairs to make a cup of coffee. This was her routine every day. A new normal.

She was trying. She was learning.

She heard Ben stir in the family room, where he usually fell asleep in his favorite recliner. Sometime last night--at least she thought it was last night--Ben had said he was going to stop drinking. She didn't really remember the conversation, and she felt it was a dream or simply wishful thinking.

She sat up in bed, swinging her legs over the side. He was actually walking around and--she inhaled deeply--was that coffee brewing? She wrapped herself in the little blanket that used to belong to her boys, and went downstairs.

Ben was standing at the sink, looking out the window.

She noticed the brewed cup of coffee next to the Keurig as he turned to her.

"Hey."

"Hey." She walked into the kitchen, just watching him.

"I made you coffee," he said with a coy smile. "I meant what I said last night. I'm done drinking."

Alice reached for the coffee mug, saying, "I've heard that one before."

"No, I really think this might be it." Alice raised her eyes to the ceiling, and took a breath.

"I'm going to go out and start planting the bulbs before the ground gets too cold."

"Want me to space them out for you?"

Alice almost dropped her coffee mug at his words. It had been a very long time since he had offered anything but advice about the planting, or anything to do with the house. He was usually too busy drinking and telling everyone else what to do.

"You want to help me, now?"

"Yeah, now. This way you will do it the right way. You know, cluster them." Alice recognized the teasing tone of his voice; a sound she hadn't heard for years.

She went upstairs to get dressed, passing on the morning shower that would usually start her day. She walked down the hall to Todd's room and leaned against the doorway, sipping coffee and feeling his presence.

"They say if you pray enough, miracles will happen," she whispered to the room, slightly raising her coffee cup. "I love you, Todd. Always and forever."

She glanced into Adam's empty room and saw the morning sun dancing off the walls.

She came back downstairs and grabbed Todd's navy blue sweatshirtsweat- shirt. Ben was already in the garage, pulling out the box of flower bulbs and taking them to the end of the driveway where Alice had planned a memory garden for Todd.

As Alice stepped out the front door, she glanced down at the corner of the steps. There he was, the little toad that somehow always seemed to appear when something new or strange was about to happen.

She glanced up at the sky, noticing the dark clouds beginning to form, and something familiar began to tickle her memory. A flash of blonde curls, and a beautiful bright smile, passed in front of her eyes, but flickered away just as quickly as it had appeared.

She glanced down at the little toad. "Shouldn't you be hibernating now?"

She heard Ben call to her and she yelled back, "I'm talking to Todd's toad. He shouldn't be out here." She turned and something floating beside her caught her eye.

A tiny white feather touched the top of the toad, then came to rest right beside it.

Alice reached down to pick it up. Another sweet, melancholy thought tickled at the edges of her memory. Raising her face to the sky, she shut her eyes and said a quick prayer. She felt something icy touch her face once, then again, and again after that. When she opened her eyes, she smiled.

It was beginning to snow.

"I guess we're doing this just in time," she called to Ben, holding the feather and walking towards him. She joined him at the end of the driveway and held out her hand to show him what she'd found.

"Look," she said, warmly. "I think an angel is smiling on us today."

A gentle wave of peace spread through her, a comfort she thought she would never feel again. She stooped beside Ben and began opening the packages of flower bulbs. Between the two of them, they would have everything planted before dark. They were going over to Adam's house for a cook-out and knew she would have time to shower before they left.

Feeling some peace for the first time since Todd died, *she knew*, today was going to be a very good day.

ABOUT THE AUTHOR

CA Coder is a lifetime resident of Northern Virginia and resides in Woodbridge with her husband. She is a retired early childhood teacher. She is involved in the community, empowering women to find their voice and realize their full potential in all areas. Her first priority is to spend time with her son, Josh, his wife and their three beautiful children that bring true joy to her again.

CA Coder has been creating stories since she was six years old. She adds an element of humor into everything she writes; she enjoys bringing her readers directly into her world and to meet her multi-dimensional characters.

Made in the USA
Middletown, DE
23 November 2019